C000259687

Praise for *The Financial Times Guide to* *and Diversity*

This is the book I was always looking for!! When I first started my I&D journey I had so many questions and this book expertly answers all of them. It lays out all the steps to build a successful I&D program in a way that is easy to understand. The mix of interviews and theory lets me know that I am not alone in what sometimes feels like a lonely path. The focus on behaviours will help I&D practitioners create safe spaces to have the hard but necessary conversations. This is the perfect companion for any I&D practitioner.

Vusa Tebe, I&D Practitioner

This book 'decodes' the very topical subject of I&D in an engaging, easy read. It not only provides loads of insights, but also great practical tips. We are living in a time of change. We need to build back better. Business has to be sustainable to survive and inclusion for all is at the heart of this. I recommend it to leaders and practitioners alike – time is ticking down to achieve the United Nations Sustainable Development Goals by 2030 where no one is left behind.

Richard Poston, CEO and Founder,
Kodiak Communications Ltd

This book is a great practical guide. It gives clear tangibles on how to take action and steps to take to make real impact. I highly recommend it to anyone looking to learn about inclusion and diversity and making a difference.

Nikki Walker, CEO, Quality Compliance Systems (QCS)

A truly inspiring read on how to drive meaningfully sustainable change by seeing diversity as the art of thinking independently together, and a sense of belonging as the heartbeat that drives inclusion. With diversity and inclusion being so imperative to personal, business, social and economic growth, I highly recommend it to anyone who is looking to get into the topic.

Caroline Frankum, CEO, Profiles Division, Kantar

Pearson

At Pearson, we believe in learning – all kinds of learning for all kinds of people. Whether it's at home, in the classroom or in the workplace, learning is the key to improving our life chances.

That's why we're working with leading authors to bring you the latest thinking and best practices, so you can get better at the things that are important to you. You can learn on the page or on the move, and with content that's always crafted to help you understand quickly and apply what you've learned.

If you want to upgrade your personal skills or accelerate your career, become a more effective leader or more powerful communicator, discover new opportunities or simply find more inspiration, we can help you make progress in your work and life.

Every day our work helps learning flourish, and wherever learning flourishes, so do people.

To learn more, please visit us at **www.pearson.com/uk**

The Financial Times

With a worldwide network of highly respected journalists, *The Financial Times* provides global business news, insightful opinion and expert analysis of business, finance and politics. With over 500 journalists reporting from 50 countries worldwide, our in-depth coverage of international news is objectively reported and analysed from an independent, global perspective.

To find out more, visit **www.ft.com**

THE FINANCIAL TIMES GUIDE TO INCLUSION AND DIVERSITY

YOUR COMPREHENSIVE GUIDE TO IMPLEMENTING A SUCCESSFUL I&D STRATEGY

VIKKI LEACH

 Pearson

Harlow, England • London • New York • Boston • San Francisco • Toronto • Sydney
Dubai • Singapore • Hong Kong • Tokyo • Seoul • Taipei • New Delhi
Cape Town • São Paulo • Mexico City • Madrid • Amsterdam • Munich • Paris • Milan

PEARSON EDUCATION LIMITED
KAO Two
KAO Park
Harlow CM17 9NA
United Kingdom
Tel: +44 (0)1279 623623
Web: www.pearson.com/uk

First edition published 2022 (print and electronic)

ISBN: 978-1-292-34104-0 (print)
         978-1-292-34102-6 (PDF)
         978-1-292-34103-3 (ePub)

British Library Cataloguing-in-Publication Data
A catalogue record for the print edition is available from the British Library

Library of Congress Cataloging-in-Publication Data

10 9 8 7 6 5 4 3 2 1
25 24 23 22 21

Cover design by At the Pop, Ltd
Cover image iStock/Getty Images Plus/Getty Images

Print edition typeset in 9.5/14pt Stone Serif ITC Pro by Straive
Printed by Ashford Colour Press Ltd, Gosport

NOTE THAT ANY PAGE CROSS REFERENCES REFER TO THE PRINT EDITION

CONTENTS

PART 3
BEHAVING AND LEADING INCLUSIVELY AS A LEADER
99

PART 4
BUILDING AN I&D APPROACH WITH LEADERS, EMPLOYEES, CUSTOMERS AND SUPPLIERS
161

ABOUT THE AUTHOR

Vikki Leach is a senior professional with extensive experience in inclusion and diversity (I&D), leading organisations and engaging business leaders to build a culturally sensitive and inclusive workplace. She is a thought leader, delivering cross-country change programmes in inclusion and behavioural change.

Vikki has widespread experience of operating in fast-changing, dynamic and results-focused businesses, delivering tangible results within timescales. Working in global matrix organisations, such as the fashion, technology and data research industries, she drives change with evidence-based data-driven conversations, mobilising teams across functional and geographical boundaries.

Vikki is a certified professional coach, with an MSc in Behavioural Change, and she is a Trustee on the board of the charity Teach Me Too.

Everyone has a talent and it is about unleashing it. Talent is more likely to be unleashed in a supportive, inclusive and empowering environment. Teams that work together outperform those that don't. Success feels better when it's shared with others.

AUTHOR'S ACKNOWLEDGEMENTS

Vusa Tebe, I&D Consultant

Sara Hill, Rolemapper

Lucy Carter, Brightworks Consultancy

Pamela Maynard, Avanade

Lisa Kepinski, Tinna Nielsen, Inclusion Nudges

Nichelle Appleby

Caroline Casey, The Valuable 500

Nat Hawley, Exceptional Individuals

Nikki Walker, More2Gain Ltd and Quality Compliance Systems (QCS)

Nikki Watkins, Tyche Consulting Ltd

PUBLISHER'S ACKNOWLEDGEMENTS

Text Credits:

6 **Ideal:** Diversity And Inclusion: A Complete Guide for HR Professionals, Mondal 2019; 6 **Government Equalities Office:** Gender pay gap, www.gov.uk 2019; 6 **Pearn Kandola LLP:** Kandola, R. S. (2009). The Value of Difference: Eliminating Bias in Organisations. United Kingdom: Pearn Kandola; 7 **Harvard Business Publishing:** Bourke, J. and Espedido, A. (2019). 'Why inclusive leaders are good for organizations and how to become one.' *Harvard Business Review*, 29 March. https://hbr.org/2019/03/why-inclusive-leaders-are-good-for-organizations-and-how-to-become-one; 7 **European Commission:** Paola Bortini, Angelica Paci, Anne Rise, Irene Rojnik, Inclusive Leadership, 2016; 25 **The Financial Times Limited:** Emma De Vita, MARCH 8 2019, Flexible working's unforeseen tensions, The Financial Times Limited; 63 **The Financial Times Limited:** Amy Bell in London MAY 31 2018, Intersectionality: look at the individual, not the minority group, The Financial Times Limited; 73 **John Wiley & Sons, Inc.:** Liswood, L. A. (2009). *The Loudest Duck: Moving Beyond Diversity While Embracing Differences to Achieve Success at Work.* Germany: Wiley; 81 **The Financial Times Limited:** Janina Conboye, 2020, 'Diversity Leaders', The Financial times Limited; 95 **Audre Lorde:** Quoted by Audre Lorde; 96 **The Financial Times Limited:** Naomi Rovnick NOVEMBER 21 2019, Health at Work, The Financial Times Limited; 97 **The Financial Times Limited:** John Thornhill NOVEMBER 26 2020, Neurodiversity can empower the workplace, The Financial Times Limited; 107 **The International Journal of Wellbeing:** Buchanan, The benefit mindset: The psychology of contribution and everyday leadership, 2017; 112 **Malini Janakiraman:** Adapted from Janakiraman, 2011 Inclusive Leadership - Critical for Competitive Advantage, See https://mobilityexchange.mercer.com/DesktopModules/DigArticle/Print.aspx?PortalId=0&ModuleId=543&Article=25; 113 **The Korn/Ferry Institute:** Zes and Landis, 2013 A better return

on self-awareness, Retrieved from https://www.kornferry.com/content/dam/kornferry/docs/article-migration/KFI-SelfAwareness-ProofPoint-6.pdf; **115 Gerald Ratner:** Quoted by Gerald Ratner; **115 Steve Easterbrook:** Quoted by Steve Easterbrook; **134 Peter Hawkins:** CLEAR Coaching Model by Peter Hawkins; **135 Jo Owen:** Global Teams' by Jo Owen, 2017; **170 Becky Johnen:** Adapted from Janakiraman, 2011 Inclusive Leadership - Critical for Competitive Advantage, Retrieved from https://mobilityexchange.mercer.com/DesktopModules/DigArticle/Print.aspx?PortalId=0&ModuleId=543&Article=25; **192 Caroline Casey:** Quoted by Caroline Casey.

FOREWORD

Pamela Maynard, CEO, Avanade

What does it take to make a space more inclusive? As a woman of colour in the tech industry, I know a thing or two about exclusive spaces. I have been the only woman or the only person of colour in a room more times than I can count. As one of the few Black female CEOs in the world, every day is an exercise in overlapping – and connecting – both identities. This intersection of identities gives me the perspective I need to build a culture of inclusivity in a room or a team or even an entire organisation.

I stepped into the role of CEO of Avanade, the leading digital innovator in Microsoft technologies, in September 2019, but inclusion and diversity have been cornerstones of the company's culture since it was founded in 2000. Our work is about innovating through the power of our people, and what is innovation about? Change. Growth. Turning something on its side and looking at it in a new way. It has been my experience that you can't innovate without diverse perspectives, and you can't be a place for diverse perspectives without an inclusive culture.

I met Vikki Leach when she joined Avanade as our director of inclusion and diversity. As the executive sponsor of our women's employee network, I saw firsthand her commitment to empowering others by creating an inclusive environment. In her introduction to this book, she writes that a leader who 'truly gets it' can be a key differentiator in unlocking inclusion and diversity. I am flattered and grateful that she sees me in this light, but it is not how I choose to see myself.

As a leader, if I think of myself as someone who 'gets it', I'm letting myself off the hook. When I became CEO of Avanade, the company had a long and rich history of prioritising I&D. We had created STEM scholarships for young women across the world, a global network of Employee Resource Groups, mentoring programmes, leadership summits, and more. To step into the role of CEO, survey the great things that had been done and say, 'We have this covered' would have been a failure of leadership. Instead, in this great responsibility, I felt a heavy knowledge that we weren't doing enough.

As we grow more intentional in our conversations about race, sex, gender and all other forms of diversity, I feel an even greater urgency. We need to make inclusion and diversity not just a business priority but a moral imperative. The state of our business, the wellbeing of our employees, and, frankly, the future of our world depends on this work. It is that important.

That is easy to say and much, much harder to do. That's why I love the functional structure of Vikki's book. I know a lot of leaders who want to do more but don't know where to start. Vikki walks you through how to conceive of inclusion and diversity, how to implement changes in meaningful ways, how to get others on board – all steps that you must take to be successful.

I&D is not meant to be a department in the corner of your company doing isolated work. It needs to be embedded into your business strategy, impacting every decision you make, felt from top to bottom. If that sounds overwhelming, that's okay. Everything begins with a step. If you're already well down the path of weaving inclusion and diversity into your business, that's wonderful, too. But remember there is always more to learn, and our capacity for innovation depends on our ability to constantly evolve. Either way, you're on the right track: You're not letting yourself off the hook.

INTRODUCTION

The business case for inclusion and diversity is becoming clearer to leaders – if they are ignoring it today, good luck to them. For a business to grow and create a sustainable future, it needs a diverse group of people, working in an inclusive environment. For these people to feel they can contribute and be included, regardless of their background, inclusive leadership is required, to drive the growth and innovation, and to do this, organisations need to bring different people together and lead in an inclusive way.

Throughout this book, I refer to inclusion (the 'I') before diversity (the 'D'). We need to start with our own behaviours and mindsets, and look to ourselves at how we behave, before we can really understand how inclusive we are prepared to be. Only then can we decide how we intend to embrace diversity as individuals.

It is far easier to build a diverse organisation from the outset than to diversify a large, complex, homogeneous machine. Start as early as you can, making it a priority in order to reap the rewards quicker. For established companies: do not put it off. The sooner you start, the sooner you make progress.

First, we need to stop and look at 'how' and 'why' the organisation is driven the way it is. Second, we need to look at 'what' we need to do about it. A leader once said to me: 'Vikki, how many lanyards do I wear to support the different diversity groups? Why can't we wear one and be proud of the behaviours and values our company holds?' Organisations spend thousands of dollars per year strategising and coming up with such company behaviours and values, but how do these really come to life? If a company says its values are inclusion and respect, how are these really brought to life? How can you live them every day? I am a believer that this starts at the top with the leaders, with employees looking up and seeing leadership behaviours brought to life and choosing to follow... or not. By getting beneath the skin of our behaviours and mindsets to simply treat people inclusively, fairly and with respect, we can begin to understand the culture of an organisation and move on to discuss 'intersectionality of the human being'.

This book gives a different perspective on behaviours, inclusion and diversity (B.I.D.). It aims to provide tools and techniques that, if your organisation is brave enough, will help shift the needle.

I find myself writing this book in one of the most uncertain and unprecedented times in my personal history. Within the last four years alone, we have observed the #metoo campaign, COVID-19 and Black Lives Matter movement.

Focus on the behaviours that impact inclusion, that embrace diversity

I have designed this book to talk to the hearts and minds of the reader and I dedicate it to all the I&D practitioners who are endlessly working to create a better environment for everyone. It is a profession that practitioners enter because they want to do good, they want to make a difference. Throughout this book, I reference the I&D practitioner because without them, this topic would not be where it is today.

If people are willing to be open-minded, look forward and create a community of inclusion and tolerance, we can move this topic on. We are in this together, it starts with us, and as soon as we recognise and learn about each other's behaviours and differences, we can look forward and create positive change together. By acknowledging and gaining this understanding, we have the opportunity to become more inclusive rather than encourage segregation.

How to use this book

The book aims to provide useful information about inclusion and diversity, giving practical tips on how to bring it to life in organisations, regardless of their size. It covers many areas of diversity, but not all, as the list is exhaustive and the topic is endless. There are four parts to the book:

Part 1 Understanding inclusion and diversity

Part 1 discusses what I&D is and the difference between inclusion and diversity. It provides information on where to start with I&D, understanding the baseline and what to work with. It moves on to discuss how to set up a structure that will begin to drive the topic forward in a practical way.

Part 2 How to put the I&D approach into practice

Part 2 discusses how to put the approach into practice and also how to embed it into the organisation's business strategy. It discusses the importance of setting targets and how to measure them. It also looks at why organisations start with gender diversity and moves on to discuss the value of Employee Resource Groups and networks.

Part 3 Behaving and leading inclusively as a leader

Part 3 looks at behaviour. This is a critical area that some organisations forget. It discusses how behaving inclusively can unlock exclusion and how powerful language can be; how our choice of language and behaviour impacts others; how we behave when working in groups; and how our behaviour changes depending on the environment we are in. It discusses how to be aware of this and respect different cultures within the groups we work in. It also discusses I&D in times of transformational change.

Part 4 Building an I&D approach with leaders, employees, customers and suppliers

Part 4 discusses how to engage leaders, raise their awareness and hold them accountable; how to attract, develop and retain diverse talent, and the implications if an organisation is not focusing on the diversity coming through its doors, and who is leaving. It also discusses how to integrate I&D into your customer and supplier efforts, and how to bring them on the journey with you.

During the writing of this book, I had the privilege of interviewing some great people I have got to know over the years, to get their perspective on I&D. This provides you with a diverse set of views along with additional tips and techniques. I have aimed to cover as much as possible, but with the topic being so broad and deep I am mindful that there may be aspects I have not included.

Also sprinkled throughout the book is the great work of Tinna Nielsen and Lisa Kepinski, in the form of 'inclusion nudges'. I am a great believer in constant nudging to make sure the topic is on the agenda of organisations to make it stick. Deploying inclusion nudges constantly throughout the year enables decision makers to be reminded of their behaviour and biases when making critical decisions about their business.

Tinna and Lisa have been providing hundreds of inclusion nudges over the past seven years to help organisations understand practically how to nudge their own behaviours and become more inclusive. Their inclusion nudges are a designed intervention based on insights from behavioural and social sciences; these gently prod the unconscious mind to change behaviour in the direction of inclusiveness by targeting the behavioural drivers, judgement and choice processes, and perceptions. Tinna and Lisa have kindly given me permission to sprinkle their great work throughout the book.

If you are lucky enough to work with an organisation where the leader 'truly gets it', this can be a key differentiator to unlocking inclusion and diversity. I have been fortunate enough to work with some leaders that truly get it, empowering me to deliver brave and bold initiatives which created real change simply because they understood the value of I&D. I have also had the pleasure of interviewing them for the book, learning what sits behind their motives. I will always be grateful to these leaders as they have been integral to my professional and personal growth, challenging me, pushing me, empowering me to be brave and to challenge the status quo.

Leaders: please set your I&D practitioner free, empower them to release their innovative ideas to be brave and bold. They are desperate to innovate and empower the organisation. They have broad skillsets because of what they do. They are expected to influence, facilitate and hold tough conversations, roll their sleeves up, offer strategic advice and navigate unhealthy behaviours, and they are at the forefront because they know what is going on beneath the surface. They are resilient and smart, pushing a tough agenda so leaders can stand on a platform and state that: 'I&D is at the heart of our business.'

'I&D is at the heart of our business.'

They do what they can to protect and promote the reputation of the organisation and the leader. I hope you enjoy the book and feel empowered by the content.

Please note, in this book I have used the binary terms of female/male, using them as a typical example. The publications in the chapter reference lists do not use non-binary examples.

Further resources

Nielsen, T. and Kepinski, L. (2016), *Inclusion Nudges Guidebook*.

PART 1
UNDERSTANDING INCLUSION AND DIVERSITY

CHAPTER 1
WHAT IS INCLUSION AND WHAT IS DIVERSITY?

What is inclusion and. . . what is diversity?

Diversity is the differences, similarities and unique characteristics in all of us. Inclusion is creating an inclusive environment regardless of different cultures, nationalities, genders, ages, thinking styles and abilities.

Diversity can be described as different groups of people from a particular culture. These groups can vary, such as: a family, a religious group, a group of people who share a similar ethnic background, life dynamics or work culture.

Because of diversity, different thinking styles and abilities will bring a broad range of approaches, and this is where the value of diversity comes in. Whether in a team or a group, different thinking styles and abilities can help get to a resolution in different ways; because of how individuals think based on their background, their thinking style may be analytical, divergent or creative. By bringing this diversity of thinking together, the richer the conversations can be in situations where solutions may need to be approached in different ways.

This book alludes to many different diversity groups, yet the topic of diversity is evolutionary and so while many groups are captured here, many more exist. It is impossible to 'box' any individual into just one diversity group. The book also discusses intersectionality, where we need to see individuals as unique human beings, giving each other respect and having the curiosity to learn about each other's differences, regardless of the diversity groups that we all belong to. In addition, the book alludes to the importance of inclusive environments for learning, in order to ensure that all voices are heard, and listened to with respect, regardless of people's backgrounds.

The pure definitions of diversity groups continue to evolve; for example, 'gender' no longer means just 'male' and 'female'. It has evolved to include non-binary terms as well as traditional binary oppositions such as male and female.

Diversity is about counting heads. Inclusion is about making heads count. Johnson (2019) attributes diversity to the physical make-up of an organisation, whereas inclusion is about how the organisation treats its people.

Why is I&D important?

Creating a diverse workforce enables an organisation to think in different ways, use different approaches, skills, experience and knowledge and build even greater success.

- By having **diverse thinking** in key decision-making roles, you can better understand your customers and employees.
- By building a **diverse workforce**, you can create greater innovation and customer awareness and increase productivity, all of which are important to any organisation that wants to remain leading edge and competitive.
- By offering employees an **inclusive place to work**, where differences are celebrated and respected, you can attract and retain great talent.
- You can provide **shareholders** with a strong combination of growth and returns.

I&D has become more visible and prominent around the world, with crises, societal campaigns and movements forcing change. Organisations are now recognising the importance of inclusion and diversity for both employee welfare and organisational performance.

When I refer to 'forcing change', I mean witnessing situations such as the COVID-19 pandemic, which pushed remote working to not being a choice but a necessity; the #metoo campaign, which brought attention to women's empowerment; and Black Lives Matter, which brought attention to Black empowerment. It is these forced changes that are needed to shake up the status quo. It is sad and unfortunate that it takes such traumatic experiences to push some organisations to recognise they need to move to action.

It is important to recognise that there is a difference between 'inclusion' and 'diversity'. Our behaviour depends on how inclusive we are; if we become inclusive in our behaviour, we can then embrace diversity. It is time that we move our conversation on and focus on our behaviour. We need to evolve our mindsets so that everyone is open and curious about each other, bringing the respect every single human being deserves.

For an organisation to be successful, inclusion and diversity need to work hand in hand to ensure employees feel valued and supported, enabling everyone to perform at their best. Society is diverse and it is important to utilise the skills of the entire population, not just a few. Evidence continues to grow to support the idea that embracing diversity simply makes business sense. Juliet Bourke's research demonstrates this (Bourke 2016, cited in Bourke and Dillon 2018).

From a financial point of view, organisations are twice as likely to meet or exceed their targets. In terms of performance, they are three times as likely to be better performing, six times more likely to be more agile and innovative and eight times more likely to have a better business outcome.

Attracting diverse groups will bring different ways of thinking and enable organisations to achieve greater success. Bourke and Dillon (2018) go on to explain that diversity of thought can enhance innovation by 20% and reduce risk by 30%.

Inclusion and diversity 'are a company's mission, strategies, and practices to support a diverse workplace and leverage the effects of diversity to achieve a competitive business advantage' (Mondal 2019: 1).

An inclusive work environment is also likely to be more attractive to younger professionals. According to Johnson (2019), this demographic will be the largest cohort of the workforce by 2025. A more diverse society is here to stay as it continues to evolve and change.

The pressure is on organisations to become more inclusive, with an expectation that their own leadership teams will invest in looking at how they behave and lead inclusively. Leaders are beginning to realise they need to raise their own awareness of how critical it is to lead inclusively and embrace diversity, bringing people together from different backgrounds, enabling them to create greater success and bring benefits to business performance. This pressure is coming from a variety of angles in society. For example, as quoted on the UK Government website: 'From 2017, any employer who has a headcount of 250 or more . . . must . . . report and publish specific figures about their gender pay gap' (GOV.UK 2020). The aim is to create fairness and equality, enabling more women to earn the same as their male counterparts. This is one example of diversity embracing inclusion.

TV advertising has become more inclusive showing different groups to help raise awareness, which is indicative of societal change. In 2019, Renault showed two same-sex partners in their advertising. Journalist Joanna Whitehead (2019) reported in *The Independent*: 'Renault Clio's new advert is a heartwarming same-sex love story set over three decades.' In 2013, Guinness showed people with disabilities in their advertising. One report stated: 'An incredible new Guinness ad breaks the industry stereotype' (Taube 2013).

Leaders are observing these movements and know they need to raise their awareness as they lead diverse groups. To support and equip leaders, a variety of training is required to help raise their own awareness of the diversity around them.

This was identified by Kandola (2009: 236): 'Awareness training can lead to an increase in knowledge and confidence in dealing with diversity issues.' Training is critical to learn about inclusive leadership, and to learn about experiences they have never lived themselves. I am a supporter of training, as long as it is delivered in a supportive way, equipping leaders in a safe space for the conversation to be put on the table. I find that one of the main sticking points is that some do not know how to talk about a topic that does not impact them. How do you get people to care about a cause when they are not impacted by it?

I allude to the example of 'if you run a marathon on a Saturday and raise money for your favourite charity, it may be because you care about that charity and have gone through an experience: you care about the cause.'

As societal pressure rises for organisations to embrace diversity and be more inclusive, a growing body of research continues to show that decision making, return on investment, innovation and the ability to capture new markets all improve when inclusive leadership is embedded in the workplace.

> Teams with *inclusive leaders* are 17% *more* likely to report that they are high performing, 20% *more* likely to say they make high-quality decisions, and 29% *more* likely to report behaving collaboratively.
>
> *(Bourke and Espedido 2019: 1, emphasis added)*

The aim of inclusive leadership is to create change and innovate while balancing everybody's needs. The key areas of development for inclusive leaders are practicing self-awareness, living a shared vision, building relationships and creating change by valuing the world they live in.

(Bortini et al. 2016: 5)

When considering inclusion and diversity, companies need to approach it as they would any other business function. As with all other functions across an organisation, it needs to be measured, targets need to be put in place, with strong business planning and strategic direction. Inclusion and diversity are no different to any other function; they need to be treated seriously and integrated into the business. The topic needs to be discussed as a business conversation.

Organisations need to map inclusion and diversity to the business and operating model. They should look to link and embed it into as many areas as possible, such as:

- business and growth strategy
- values/behaviours
- purpose
- vision
- mission statement
- organisational policies
- leadership development programmes.

Inclusion and diversity cannot be a stand-alone. It is not separate to organisational performance. It is not just about 'doing the right thing'. It makes business sense. If managed well it can contribute to higher performance and higher profitability. This is because any organisation, as it faces accelerating transformation pressure, will require strong, agile leaders to foster an inclusive behaviour and leadership style, where a wide range of backgrounds, styles and thinking are able to come together to inspire its clients and customers.

If an organisation wants to create growth, it will need to differentiate. To differentiate it will require innovation and to innovate it needs diversity. To activate this diversity, it needs inclusion and to manage all of this it will need to ensure inclusive leadership is in place.

This can be achieved if the organisation takes a bold step and starts to generate increasing numbers of diverse leaders in order to build an attractive place to work, so that it reflects its customers and communities. Here are some questions to start the discussion in your organisation:

1   **How brave is your organisation prepared to be?** The braver your organisation is, the better, as you will see stronger results.

2   **Does the organisation want to be on an external platform talking about the topic, be known for inclusion and diversity efforts, or simply comply?** Decide whether you want to be humble and aspirational or an activist. Just make sure you have good results and strong case studies if you become an activist.

3   **What is your organisation ready for?** Your organisation can no longer do nothing. It needs to be ready for change. Identify what that change should be and why it's necesssary.

4   **Where are you now versus where you want to get to?** Use a maturity model and decide your position.

The first step is to be honest about the commitment your organisation is willing to make with inclusion and diversity.

Further resources

Bortini, P., Paci, A., Rise, A. and Rojnik, I. (2016). *Inclusive Leadership: Theoretical Framework.* http://inclusiveleadership.eu/the-inclusive-leadership-handbook-theoretical-framework/

Bourke, J. and Dillon, B. (2018). 'The diversity and inclusion revolution'. *Deloitte Review*, Issue 22, January, pp. 81–95. https://www2.deloitte.com/content/dam/insights/us/articles/4209_Diversity-and-inclusion-revolution/DI_Diversity-and-inclusion-revolution.pdf

Bourke, J. and Espedido, A. (2019). 'Why inclusive leaders are good for organizations and how to become one'. *Harvard Business Review*, 29 March. https://hbr.org/2019/03/why-inclusive-leaders-are-good-for-organizations-and-how-to-become-one

GOV.UK (2020). 'Guidance: Who needs to report their gender pay gap?', 14 December 2020, updated 23 February 2021. https://www.gov.uk/guidance/who-needs-to-report-their-gender-pay-gap

Johnson, J. (2019). 'Why inclusion is good for business, and how it differs from diversity'. *Orlando Business Journal*, 16 April. https://www.bizjournals.com/orlando/news/2019/04/16/why-inclusion-is-good-for-business-and-how-it.html

Kandola, B. (2009). *The Value of Difference: Eliminating Bias in Organisations*. Pearn Kandola Publishing.

McKinsey & Co and Lean In (2019). 'Women in the workplace 2019'. https://leanin.org/women-in-the-workplace-2019

Mondal, S. (2019). *Diversity & Inclusion: A Beginner's Guide for HR Professionals*. https://ideal.com/diversity-and-inclusion/.

Taube, A. (2013). 'An incredible new Guinness ad breaks the industry stereotype'. *Business Insider*, 5 September. https://www.businessinsider.in/advertising/an-incredible-new-guinness-ad-breaks-the-industry-stereotype/articleshow/22348870.cms

Whitehead, J. (2019). 'Renault Clio's new advert is a heartwarming same-sex love story set over three decades'. *The Independent*, 12 November.

CHAPTER 2
HOW TO UNDERSTAND THE BASELINE FOR I&D

In this chapter we will focus on how to understand the I&D baseline, where you are now and the existing internal policies and processes you have in place. It is important to identify your current position, then you can decide where to focus your efforts.

A good place to start is to undertake an audit across your organisation. This will enable you to identify the problems and the gaps, helping you to build a plan.

The audit

Having the evidence and data is critical to start. Most organisations are data driven, so collecting evidential data will enable you to understand where you currently are, but do accept that you may not be able to obtain everything you need. The data collection will only be as good as the systems you have in place and also the legal standpoint of the data you are allowed to collect. This varies from country to country.

Data and diagnostics

I discussed data and diagnostics with Lucy Carter from Brightworks Consultancy. Lucy explains where to start.

Vikki: *Lucy, why do organisations come to you in the first place – what are they looking to do?*

Lucy: *Organisations contact us to help them create inclusion and diversity strategies and plans for many reasons, usually because their board and senior team are pushing for change, because they are legally required to do so or their engagement survey suggests some challenges. Rarely is the request driven by their own data. Unless the organisation is focused on creating a diverse and inclusive place to work, they do not tend to be collecting and analysing much relevant information. Definitely a chicken and egg scenario.*

Our recommendation to almost all clients therefore is to start with data and diagnostics. It is easy to look at the senior team or across your colleagues and see a lack of diversity but until you dive into your employee data you do not know for sure what is going on, if there is an imbalance, where that is and where it might be coming from. It is only when you start to get a handle on these questions that you can even think about strategies for change.

Vikki: *What kind of data should they look for?*

Lucy: *One of the first barriers we meet with clients is 'we do not collect any inclusion and diversity data'. What that often means is that they do not collect, and store, new and existing employee demographics as regards to gender, age, ethnicity, ability, religion or sexual orientation, which may well be true for many (most) organisations. In addition, for global teams, legislation will prevent the capture, storage and analysis of the data for some or all of these dimensions in some locations.*

For many organisations, however, there will most likely be some data you can access which can start to build a picture of what is happening. We see data and diagnostic work as acting like a funnel. The initial stage at the top is all about looking for any quantitative data available and creating a baseline where you can start to make some hypotheses about what is going on and identify areas or aspects of the organisation that are worthy of some extra deep dive. You can also identify data gaps at this stage which can form part of the action planning itself. Any hypotheses can then be tested with further qualitative work like surveys, groups or interviews to identify key challenges and therefore potential strategic options.

As a starting point many organisations capture gender information (often still just male/female/prefer not to say) and age at least. Global teams may collect other data according to the laws of each of their countries. So, if this is what you have available, why not start here.

So as an example, we work with many organisations who want to improve their gender balance and so the first data we will be looking for is gender splits. However, what they often mean is that they are not seeing enough women coming through to the senior level and so gender splits would not be enough. So, we need to try and access gender data by levels, teams, regions, functions. Straight away, even if you do not do anything else, you may be able to see a diversity chal-lenge and something to work on. Do proportions of women drop off at certain levels, managerial or leadership, for example? Are you see-ing an imbalance in particular teams, at certain levels in particular teams, in certain functions in particular regions etc.?

This data tends to be the most readily available and by cutting it in these ways you have a good starting point to make some hypotheses to test by further quantitative or qualitative work. If you have any employee data regarding other diversity dimensions, then you can analyse it in the same way.

Now it is important to recognise that seeing imbalance at this stage is not necessarily a problem for your organisation. The proportions may well reflect national population averages or recognised global challenges, for example the lack of women in certain professions. The data is part of a story that can be tested through further diag-nostic work and can help you agree priorities.

Vikki: *What other quantitative data can be helpful?*

Lucy: *Beyond any basic employee demographics, if your organisation holds data supporting people processes this can provide a rich seam for investigation. For example:*

Recruitment: Starting with recruitment, the ideal scenario is the collection of candidate demographic data throughout the recruit-ment funnel, for example at attraction, application, screening, assessment, offer, start stages. Recruitment funnel data is key as it helps to pinpoint if and at which stage there may be any bias occur-ring. Adverse impact analysis identifies whether there is a marked difference in proportions of one group over another as candidates progress through the recruitment process.

If this process is not followed, what is collected by your organisation and when? Do you at least collect gender data, and can you see any differences in the pattern of applicants to new starters, for example? Can you look at this data for different levels, teams, regions and functions again to identify any patterns or anomalies?

Some organisations have moved to a practice of taking off demographic information at the early stages of recruitment to try and reduce bias so this would restrict the pattern analysis.

Performance and promotion: *Even more important to the landscape is the progression of existing employees up through the organisation. Identifying who is and who is not being promoted, in what teams, at what levels, in what regions and how that compares to any performance data provides a useful indicator. Does promotion correlate with high performance or is there something else going on in the promotion process?*

You may not have 'promotion' data, but you might be able to identify when levels of employees change, if you record levels on the database.

Leavers: *On the other end of the employee journey, you may well have data about those leaving your organisation. Again, look for any patterns, at levels, regions, teams, functions. Can you identify any particular groups of people who are leaving at a greater proportion than starting or are over-indexing as leavers?*

This data can be supplemented by exit interview data – does your organisation conduct these? Do you record reasons for leaving or anything else from the interview? The leaver data can potentially be brought to life with the lived experiences of employees.

Bringing it all together: *Bringing new starter, progression and leaver data together can be exceptionally illuminating in what we describe as an 'Ins, Ups and Outs' movement of talent diagnostic tool. It provides a really rich overview of what is happening in an organisation. We have created these to show what is happening between genders, for example in organisations as they progress* *through its hierarchical levels. It may help you to identify possible drivers for your generic splits recognised at the start. It can show you where you may have 'leaky pipelines', for example where a greater proportion of a group are leaving rather than starting or being promoted up a level. You might also be able to spot 'glass ceilings' or 'sticky floors' where groups of employees get stuck at particular levels and do not appear to be able to progress or leave, either driven by bias in the talent management processes or lack of confidence, support and/or information to push further. The McKinsey & Co and Lean In study (2019) identified 'broken rungs' at first-level management preventing women from reaching the top.*

Identifying these potential situations will not give you any reasons why but will help you decide who to talk to when you are moving on to the qualitative stages and what kind of questions to ask.

Other data communities: *If data collection and/or storage is not widespread, you may find you can look at particular communities. Your 'talent pools', for example – those employee groups who are considered to be the leaders of the future, such as senior leadership teams, high potential groups, graduate or apprenticeship groups. Who are in these groups and are they representative of the wider population? It is also worth looking at how you identify such 'talent'. We have compared performance ratings of men versus women at the higher levels of organisations and in some, while women tended to perform better on average, there were higher proportions of men in the 'talent' and 'senior leadership' groups. So perhaps some organisations value something other than, or additional to, 'high performance' to be classed as 'talent' or there is something else at work?*

Other data sources: *There are other less obvious data sources which can be indicative of cultural responses to inclusion and diversity.*

Any flexible/agile working pattern data can be useful. We know that the ability to have some control over pattern of work has a definite link to the progression of women into senior roles and introducing flexibility remains a high priority for organisations who are focused on gender equality. Remote working or flexible hours can also be particularly attractive for people with disabilities and/or caring responsibilities and older and younger candidates. So, it is worth looking at any data on working patterns or at least contract types, such as part-time versus full-time. Where are the part-time employees working? Just the lower levels, in certain teams, in certain locations? And what happens to them? Do they progress at the same rate as full-time employees do? How do their performance ratings compare? Are they included in any of the talent groups? This can help you build hypotheses about whether part-time employees are valued as much and whether a part-time role is judged as a job or a career worth progressing and therefore the implications for the groups who look for flexibility.

Maternity and paternity/family leave data is often collected by organisations and can add to the inclusion picture. From a data perspective:

- *have a look at the proportion of employees taking leave versus national averages*
- *evaluate proportions of returners and stayers.*

If there are comparably low levels of take-up, return or longer-term retention, this might indicate some challenges around support, opportunity and organisational culture that could be worth investigating more.

So, you can see here that you do not have to have a full demographic data set to get going on trying to identify what is happening in your organisation. The ability to layer and compare different analyses will help you to start to create a story and hypotheses to test further. Also, it is a huge generalisation to suggest that if an organisation is imbalanced for one particular dimension of diversity it will follow for others, and it is not right to cluster different communities together. However, if an organisation is focused on creating a culture and people processes which are more inclusive to all, then it is more likely to become more diverse over time. Therefore, whatever data you can collect and analyse, it helps to build the picture!

Vikki: *So, what can they do with the data?*

Lucy: *Any data you are able to collect can be analysed to look for patterns or anomalies and used to build some hypotheses, with caveats over sample size or data gaps. The data can also indicate areas worth more investigation. This could be areas showing very little diversity or areas which appear more balanced or perhaps areas with very little data at all.*

Because inclusion and diversity sit at the centre of organisational culture and employee experience, to really make sense of the data you need input from employees themselves. It is not just a numbers game. How you do that depends on the size and structure of organisation and resources available.

Listening to people about their lived experience in this area is very personal and often quite emotional because it touches on the very heart of identity and any struggles or bias experienced. So where possible, and I suggest where you identify any really challenging areas, conduct completely confidential one-to-one interviews. This is the only way to properly hear and explore employee experiences and I would always recommend external support who can guarantee that confidentiality. Talk to as many colleagues as you can afford to, across regions, teams, levels and functions, but ensure you focus your efforts on some of the areas you have identified as potential challenges and on members of diverse communities.

Interview questions can be informed by what you might have learnt from the data but should focus on experience at work and development opportunities, the culture of the organisation and the team, what it takes to get ahead and any barriers to progress, ambitions and awareness of how to progress. You can also ask more specifically about any inclusion and diversity practices or activity if that is relevant.

Also, interview a sample of managers and senior team members with similar questions. It is good to include their views but also to see if there is any difference with the wider employee population.

Focus groups can be useful also but they are more suited to less personal and more generic areas of discussion like flexible working or maternity/family leave experiences where guaranteed anonymity is perhaps not as important.

From both the interviews and focus groups you can identify themes for particular employee groups and also pull out specific (but *anonymous) stories as illustrations. You can use these themes and stories to either provide some rationale to the data/identified challenges or perhaps to question the original data, as you may find that the culture is changing and the demographics of the employees have not yet caught up.*

For the most robust responses you could add a wider employee survey. These can work in different ways. Some organisations send out diversity monitoring surveys to their employees. While this is completely voluntary and return levels may be quite low, employees are more likely to engage with this exercise if they see it as a valuable part of the strategy for promoting inclusivity.

If you have an ongoing employee survey tool, you can add in questions which will help you assess how inclusive the working environment is, and you can slice the response data into different areas such as job level, region and business unit.

Alternatively, you could send a bespoke survey to all employees or a representative sample. Responses to these will obviously not be at the depth of the interviews. But with this or the employee survey, you can cross-tabulate responses with the relevant original data points identified to assess the scale of any challenges and create real actionable insight.

Vikki: *What can all this data show me?*

Lucy: *Obviously collecting data on its own cannot drive change so choosing what to use the data for is what is important.*

Bringing everything together, you may identify whether there are potential barriers to the progress of different groups of people in your organisation and therefore challenges to inclusivity. This might be about culture and leadership, messaging and communications, specific people processes such as recruitment, talent management, performance management, learning and development or working practices, for example.

It is at this point you can start to create a strategy to address these with objectives and plans. A key part of this should be introducing tools to collect, store and track data and a focus on filling the data gaps where possible, so that over time you can build that knowledge and drive and measure change.

In summary:

- Find out what data you are able to collect.

- Create a baseline and hypothesis.

- Slice the data in as many ways as you can to find the barriers – such as job level, gender, regions, functions.

- Identify your data gaps.

- Work with the data (qualitative and quantitative) you have and find ways (where possible) to collect the data you do not have.

- Identify who is leaving, joining and being promoted.

- Build your plan based on your findings.

- Identify a balanced view – that is, the challenges versus the opportunities.

Moving forward with the data and diagnostics

Strategically you want to understand whether your organisation has or is willing to include inclusion and diversity in its strategic planning. For example, is it discussed in:

- business plans

- communications/marketing strategy

- customer strategy

- country/sector strategy?

Check that company **statements**, such as the following, include inclusion and diversity:

- mission

- vision

- purpose

- company metrics

- people/talent plan

- policies

- goals/targets

- company values.

Look at the **customer/client** offering. Does it have inclusion and diversity in its design processes, such as:

- customer intelligence
- product innovation
- research and development
- client discussions?

As Lucy mentioned, employee engagement surveys are useful for understanding the baseline. They enable an organisation to find out how their employees are feeling and what they are experiencing. These surveys have the purpose of improving employee engagement, and the questions you include will provide you with good insight. They will help you scope out areas of improvement and you can track the questions over time.

You want to seek out questions that relate to inclusion and diversity. Table 2.1 gives some examples of questions that may be asked.

On extracting the data, you can cluster responses, for example pulling together 'strongly agree' and 'agree', which will give you a percentage of employees who are generally positive about the questions.

Clustering 'disagree' and 'strongly disagree' will give an indication of those employees who are not having a positive experience.

Policies

An audit of your policies is a big task but one worth starting with to determine your baseline. Policies play a critical role in employee welfare and creating an inclusive environment. Organisations need policies to set standards and build inclusivity among their diverse workforce. Policies help people understand their rights and the organisation's position on specific aspects.

When auditing a policy, it is best to engage with a few employees (qualitative data) as to how the policy affects them. You can gather a small group of employees and have a discussion on the effectiveness of the policy, helping you better understand what might be missing from it. You will be able to determine whether the organisation is complying with the law on specific policies or whether it is more generous by providing extra benefits. For example, offering

Table 2.1 Example questions in an employee engagement survey

Inclusion questions	Results
My company takes an interest in my wellbeing	● Strongly Agree ● Agree ● Neutral ● Disagree ● Strongly Disagree
I feel included in my team	● Strongly Agree ● Agree ● Neutral ● Disagree ● Strongly Disagree
In my team we have different types of skills and people from different backgrounds	● Strongly Agree ● Agree ● Neutral ● Disagree ● Strongly Disagree
In my team, my manager ensures that all our voices are heard, and valued	● Strongly Agree ● Agree ● Neutral ● Disagree ● Strongly Disagree
My company embraces diversity by employing, developing and retaining a mix of talent	● Strongly Agree ● Agree ● Neutral ● Disagree ● Strongly Disagree

additional parental leave over and above the statutory requirement a country stipulates can give a competitive edge with attracting and retaining talent. Employees will sometimes move to another organisation because its policies, such as healthcare benefits, are more generous.

During the audit, you may look at how inclusive the language is. For example, moving from 'maternity and paternity' leave to 'primary and secondary care givers' leave, the language becomes more inclusive and employees may feel more comfortable in requesting the different types of leave they need. If employees are not represented in a policy, they will experience exclusion.

Flexible working

As Lucy points out above, flexible working is a huge topic, and one worth auditing as a priority, as it touches on many aspects of work/life demands and performance. You can identify whether there are biases or assumptions made, such as whether the policy is biased towards working mothers who need to juggle their work and home life. A flexible working policy goes well beyond this. In today's world, there is a long list of employees who require some form of flexibility because of the demands that life now puts on us all, for example:

● caring responsibilities for different family members

● ability (physical/mental) and individual needs

● childcare for primary and secondary care givers.

Since the COVID-19 pandemic, working conditions have drastically changed, but attitudes may not have. You may want to check with employees, regardless of the policy in place, whether they really experience – and are treated – with respect and fairness when working flexibly. Flexibility is not just about working part time; it is exactly what it states – 'working flexibly' – and it needs to be inclusive to all employees. The focus groups will help you determine whether there is a culture of trust when employees work flexibly, regardless of whether they deliver on their objectives. It will help you understand whether the organisation is measuring the performance of its employees, rather than how many hours they are working in a week.

I spoke about this topic with Nikki Walker, the Chief Executive Officer (CEO) of the UK's largest provider of compliance policies, procedures and guidance, Quality Compliance Systems (QCS), which knits process with clarity as standard. Nikki talked about the journey QCS is on to offer flexible working properly, the importance of accountability and of being systematic in your approach.

Vikki: *Nikki, where did you start with your journey to flexible working?*

Nikki: *Three years ago, employees were focussed on hours worked rather than results delivered. Everyone was at their desks all day, but half the time they were not focussed on work. I would say: 'We are judging people on how long they are sitting at their desk. We need to shift to judging people on what they deliver.' Measuring the hours people work is not the important piece; it has got to be all about results.*

You need to have the right accountability in place: People have to be really clear what they are responsible for achieving. Having this in place builds a culture of trust and ensures people are clear on what success looks like in a positive way. If managers are not physically with their teams, they have got to trust them to deliver the results needed and know that they are because the right accountability is in place.

Visibility is central to building trust: We use the Entrepreneurial Operating System® which is a simple set of tools and a proven process to produce powerful business results. We have a three-year plan and a ten-year vision. We also have a communication strategy, which emphasises our core values making sure people understand what their role is. Crucially, it ensures that people understand their role, and how it fits in with others. It is not perfect but it provides people with clarity as to what they need to do in a week and a quarter. It is also visible so everybody can see what everybody else is delivering.

I did not introduce 'Everyday Flex' to be nice. My view has always been the same. If we, as a company, can give people a choice as to how and when they work, then they will be happier. They are also likely to stay with QCS for longer. A happy fully engaged team helps accelerate growth.

It is really important leaders role model that they are living flexibly: We cannot just 'talk the talk'; we have to 'walk the walk'. Our teams take their cues from the way we behave. One of the things I always do is put personal commitments into my diary, whether that is going to the hairdressers or taking time out for a run. I share with people where I will be because I want them to know that it is okay to take time to do things that are important to us and to balance work with life.

We introduced Everyday Flex in November 2020. It was a natural transition for the team because we had done a lot of work leading up to it, asking people what their concerns were, how they thought they would overcome any challenges and what coping strategies could be put in place. We actually could not believe how easy it was. We were so pleased that everyone embraced it so well and so quickly.

You need to have an equal playing field: We agreed as a senior team that we all had to embrace the move to more flexibility and that all teams would have the same rules. Everybody signed up to that. Our teams watched us start to live a more flexible work life and they embraced it too. Some people I would never have imagined could be more productive once they were away from the distractions of the office suddenly became even more effective.

Vikki: *Would you ever go back?*

Nikki: *We definitely will not go back to where we were. We are hiring more and more people based right across the UK which has opened up a much larger talent pool to us. We have got people literally scattered all over the country now. We will still have office space in the future but I think it will be mainly for collaboration and ensuring we maintain human relationships. I do not foresee a time we will mandate that people have to come into the office apart from periodically to maintain relationships and for company meetings.*

The link between flexible working and productivity

Vikki: *Does the ability to work flexibly make you more productive?*

Nikki: *Yes, research suggests that this is the case. A 2014 survey by BT found that the productivity of flexible workers increased by 30 per cent (Unison and Working Families 2014). Similarly, a YouGov survey from 2015 suggested that 30 per cent of office workers felt their productivity increased when they worked remotely. In a study of flexible workers undertaken by Cranfield University, over 90 per cent of managers said the quantity and quality of work improved or stayed the same (Working Families and Cranfield University 2008).*

Flexible working and the COVID-19 pandemic

According to global technology company Cisco (2020), remote working during the pandemic has challenged society's cultural norms around the workplace:

- 87 per cent of office workers want the ability to choose whether to work from home or office, and manage their hours, even when offices open up.
- 63 per cent want to maintain the autonomy they experienced during the pandemic lockdown.

- Experiencing better balance of life around work, 54 per cent were able to incorporate more exercise into their daily routine.

- If they were CEO for a day, 79 per cent would prioritise ensuring effective collaboration and communication in the new world of work.

There is a broad range of evidence stating that flexibility is critical to modern life. For example, Emma De Vita, writing in the 'Women in business' section of the *Financial Times* (2019), quotes from the charity Working Families: 'There is evidence that people who are working part-time and flexibly can be among the most productive people in an organisation.'

Company travel

COVID-19 aside, some employees are required to travel with their role, sometimes extensively. Look at the company travel policy, and investigate how inclusive it is. Some organisations have a policy in place that recognises the challenges for some employees who are required to travel for their role and adds guidelines that might be seen to be more empathic, such as: 'primary and secondary care givers are required to travel five overnights a quarter'.

Activating policies

It is good to have policies, but if they sit dormant and are not activated then they are not adding value to employee engagement or benefits. When reviewing policies as part of the audit, you may want to test how often they are activated, for example misconduct, inappropriate behaviour etc. What are the consequences behind these? Do the policies state 'zero tolerance' and, if so, has this been carried through when the policy has had to be activated? This can be discussed with the legal and/or compliance team – they will be able to explain the action taken against the policy rules. It is important to challenge the organisation's thinking on this. For example, if its best salesperson has been bullying employees, is the organisation prepared to dismiss its top salesperson?

You may wish to look at fairness in the policies. For example, if an employee is out of the business for a long period of time, a common question is: how does an organisation treat the bonus pool? What is the policy around bonus and performance ratings distribution for that employee? Look at whether the employee has a form of pro rata on their bonus while they are on leave of absence. For example, if an employee was to be out of the business for 100 days, would they receive 265/365 of their bonus?

Undertaking a thorough review of this type of policy, especially with women in mind who have been/are on career leave, may give you some telling answers. If examples such as this one are not considered and women fall behind on pay, promotional opportunities etc., this will have an impact on other areas you will be auditing such as gender pay gap. Ensure you look at the review and whether the approach stated is fair. For example, you may read:

- **It is at the discretion of the manager** – be mindful that if training is not provided, the manager may hold a bias and approach the process unfairly.

- **A bonus and/or performance rating** is given for the entire year regardless of career leave.

- **A bonus and/or performance rating** is given the same as the previous year, preventing an employee from receiving a lower one.

Whichever approach is selected, the aim is to remove any bias from the policy, enabling managers to be fair and consistent and not exclude those who take a career break.

During the audit, have a look at 'narrow language', such as gender pronouns. Gender pronouns are words that an individual would like others to use when talking about them. Common pronouns include: 'he, him, his'/'she, her, hers'. Some individuals may choose non-binary pronouns such as 'they, them, theirs'. By just using binary language, it may exclude a portion of your workforce.

Your aim is to have I&D 'everywhere', across all policies, practices and conversations. As you discover your baseline as a result of your audit, observe how much I&D is present in everything you have reviewed and audited. If it is not present, it is not being spoken about.

In addition to policies, audit current guidelines. These will be tools and resources that equip managers to deal with situations. Awareness and education are needed in order for them to deal with the policies, so ensure you audit any training that has/has not been provided to those who will need to act on the policies.

Once you have undertaken an audit, you will be in a stronger position to decide where you are as a baseline. You may also want to take an external audit, to see how you compare against other organisations in your sector, or outside your sector.

Kantar, a data, analytics and consulting company, has developed the Inclusion Index with a mission to enable organisations to understand, track and measure their own progress in developing an inclusive and diverse workplace on a global scale. The beauty of benchmarking is that it provides an unbiased perspective on what 'good' looks like and enables development of an actionable roadmap. The audit covers a range of experiences and sentiment; it is a questionnaire that is split into five key sections. A library of questions are fed into each section based on region.

1   **Demographics:** Based on country; asks respondent if they wish to self-identify on key diversity dimensions

2   **Core questions:** Covers actions that are being taken by the company to address inclusion and diversity; it asks about existing policies in place

3   **Questionnaire:** Asks about sentiment regarding company culture as it relates to inclusion and diversity

4   **Behaviour:** Behaviour observed and experienced in the company

5   **Additional questions:** such as flexible working, health and wellness

Once you have gained data from the audits you have undertaken, the next step is to look at a maturity model alongside the plan you intend to build. It is a good exercise to present this to your organisation and have the conversation about where you are currently at (based on your audit) and where you want to move to. Table 2.2 is an example of a maturity model showing how you can discuss the different stages you can move through and how far your organisation is prepared to go. Ensure a timeline is considered when having your discussion, so that moving through the stages becomes realistic and achievable.

An organisation must first have an honest conversation and discuss its own ambitions. You may wish to be humble, yet aspirational, agreeing to remain as a beginner for a long period of time, whether it is six months or six years, or move to being a performer over a similar timeline. The most important thing is that everyone is in agreement about where you want to get to and over what timeline. The organisation needs to recognise the consequences of its decision – for example, if its remains a beginner for a long period of time, you need to

Table 2.2 An example of a maturity model

Beginner	Aware	Leader	Champion
Recognise the value of inclusion and diversity, provide information to stakeholders and value other opinions.	Work effectively to bring together individuals with diverse perspectives and skills to achieve inclusivity.	Create an environment where inclusion and diversity are recognised, valued and promoted, reaching out to all stakeholder groups, reaching and/or exceeding targets.	Champions inclusion and diversity across the organisation, putting inclusive behaviours at the heart of everything: among peers, teams and customers.

recognise what your competitors are doing and the expectations your employees and customers have.

Whichever level you select, ensure there is the commitment and drive behind your ambition in order to deliver against it. Reputationally you want to be able to deliver on what you declare to your employees, customers and other stakeholders. By deciding your position based on the maturity model, and putting a timeline against your ambition, you can make sure you are being realistic. Recognise that your efforts and progress will take time. Achieving 'champion' could take years.

To use the maturity model, you may wish to make a list under each box, determining what it means for your organisation. Identify progress so you know when and how you get there. For example:

Beginner: Recognise the value of inclusion and diversity; provide information to stakeholders and value other opinions.

- Produce an I&D annual report declaring intended commitment and progress to date.
- Begin to talk about I&D in meetings, bringing opinions together and valuing them, and understanding what it means to each other.
- Introduce a communication strategy that encourages conversations on I&D, such as an employee social media tool.
- Begin to talk about I&D in leader's speeches to employees, stakeholders, shareholders, customers and clients etc.

Aware: Work effectively to bring together individuals with diverse perspectives and skills to achieve inclusivity.

- Strengthen the understanding of I&D and how it is important to the organisation.
- Begin to look at how your organisation is bringing people from different backgrounds together to embrace different skillsets.
- Look at the talent process and how you:
  - attract diversity
  - develop diversity
  - retain diversity.
- Launch a few policy initiatives that you have audited and improved, showing employees that you are committed to making policies more inclusive.

Leader: Create an environment where inclusion and diversity are recognised, valued and promoted, reaching out to all stakeholder groups, exceeding targets.

- Place accountability on leaders to take executive sponsorship roles, so they become active in the conversation and show support to diverse groups.
- Promote and recognise diverse groups who have come together, creating a safe space for employees.
- Set bold targets, not just easy ones that are easily achievable.
- Partner with external organisations, for example the fashion industry, making a commitment to be more representative of diverse groups in clothing, styling, modelling etc., thus becoming more inclusive and accessible.
- Bring up I&D in as many conversations as possible across the organisation, from team meetings to speeches.
- Ensure there is diverse representation at every level, not just at job levels lower down the organisation, but at leadership levels and in key decision-making roles.

Champion: Champion inclusion and diversity across the organisation, putting inclusive behaviours at the heart of everything: among peers, teams and clients.

- Ensure I&D is discussed everywhere – for example, begin all meetings with a quick check-in around inclusivity.

- Take a stand in your industry; call out strong commitments that champion inclusion.
- Have the conversation with your clients and customers.
- Test your products and services for inclusion and diversity.
- Be inclusive in your marketing and communication strategies.
- Include the topic in key decision-making environments such as board meetings, shareholder meetings etc.
- Create partnerships and audit your supply chain management; identify how diverse it is.

To match the audit with a maturity model, you can identify where to start. You may find that you are on the starting block ('beginner') and you want to move to 'champion' over the next 18 months.

Ensure you have the agreement from key decision makers that 'champion' is where you want to aim for over the timeline identified. It is important to get approval and commitment and it is valuable to identify a sponsor at leadership level to support the commitment, holding them accountable.

Assessing the current situation and making a formal commitment to what your ambition is will give you a strong start to move to action. The commitment needs to be thought through based on your organisation's footprint, for example different countries, cultures and operations. This will also have to take into account the different legislation and standards across different geographies.

Undertaking an audit is a big task. The deeper you go, the richer the insight you will have. Slice the data and gather the information in as many ways as you can, as this will get you beneath the surface and identify what needs to be done. Go through the data with others, as they may find different things, they may see things differently and read things differently from you. This is the value of having a diverse set of eyes on your findings.

Further resources

Interviews

Lucy Carter, Director at Brightworks Consultancy.

Nikki Walker, Managing Director of More2Gain Ltd and Chief Executive Officer at Quality Compliance Systems (QCS).

Publications

Cisco (2020). *Employee Ownership and Choice in a New World: Workforce of the Future Survey 2020*. https://ebooks.cisco.com/story/workforce-of-the-future/page/1?ccid=cc001980&oid=ebkco023467

Financial Times (2019). 'Flexible working's unforeseen tensions', Emma De Vita, 8 March.

McKinsey & Co and Lean In (2019). 'Women in the workplace 2019'. https://leanin.org/women-in-the-workplace-2019

Unison and Working Families (2014). *Flexible Working: Making it Work*. https://www.unison.org.uk/content/uploads/2014/09/On-line-Catalogue225422.pdf

Working Families and Cranfield University (2008). *Flexible Working and Performance: Summary of Research*. https://www.workingfamilies.org.uk/wp-content/uploads/2014/09/Flexible-Working-Performance-2008.pdf

YouGov (2015). '30% of UK office workers are more productive when working remotely', 20 October. https://yougov.co.uk/topics/politics/articles-reports/2015/10/20/30-uk-office-workers-are-more-productive-when-work

CHAPTER 3
HOW TO SET UP A STRUCTURE FOR I&D

Now the baseline has been identified, you can create a structure to ensure you have the right approach, with resource and a direction in place. In this chapter we will discuss how to do this. Setting up an I&D structure will include different elements that need to be considered to enable it to have a strong position within the organisation.

The I&D practitioner

An organisation is likely to create a 'Head of I&D', to lead the topic. Ideally, the role will report directly to the CEO and hold the position of a 'Chief Diversity Officer', with a seat on the board and advise the CEO along with the board members. This gives it gravitas and the perception of commitment by the organisation. Do not underestimate how this will be observed by employees, customers, clients and other stakeholders. They will see that the organisation is really committed.

There are a range of articles written where CEOs talk about why it takes so long for change to happen. I believe this comes back to the empowerment the Head of I&D (the I&D practitioner) has or does not have. I&D will be adopted slowly if it is not taken seriously and is a side thought, and if the I&D practitioner does not have access to leaders.

In an anonymous interview with an experienced I&D practitioner, I raised this subject of 'buy-in':

Vikki: *As an I&D practitioner in a large global organisation, you tirelessly drive the agenda in an environment where you are trying to create change. What are your biggest challenges and how can your efforts be made easier?*

Anon I&D practitioner: *The biggest challenge I face as a practitioner is that people often view I&D as something 'extra' or separate to their day-to-day work. They always ask me what they need to 'do', as if I can provide a checklist of actions that they can tick off and move on.*

What many people fail to see is that I&D has to be integrated into their core role and their everyday behaviours in the workplace. They need to take a strategic approach, and understand how everything, from the systems and processes they are building and interacting with, to engaging with fellow colleagues, clients and other stakeholders, requires a commitment to behaving inclusively and ensuring people of all backgrounds are represented. 'Doing' I&D is not just taking one-off training, or attending an event, and then continuing as normal.

In order to make I&D efforts easier, companies need to clearly articulate their expectations when it comes to inclusive behaviours, and effectively communicate these to all employees – not just via official policies such as codes of conduct, but through a variety of channels including onboarding and training programmes, appraisals and performance management systems, as well as reiterating them in all employee communications. When behaviours are clearly communicated and modelled throughout the business, employees will really understand what I&D looks like, and how to do it.

Many I&D practitioner roles are placed in HR, which can also be a good decision as it is linked to talent, performance, recruitment, reward, employee relations and many other components an HR function provides. The danger is that stakeholders will see it as another HR activity; nevertheless, if it is in HR, the key is to move the topic through HR and out into the business, enabling everyone to understand that it is a business imperative, linking it to performance and profitability.

Whether the 'Head of I&D' role sits in HR, ideally reporting into the Chief People Officer (usually head of HR), or reports directly into the CEO, once this is established the Head of I&D needs to be operating at a level advising the most senior leaders. The role must have access to information, data and its people. Ideally the role does not want to be lower than the two reporting lines suggested here.

The role is challenging and it is important to appoint a strong individual with deep subject-matter expertise to bring leaders and stakeholders on the journey of change.

Much of the role is also about change management. It is not fair on the organisation or the practitioner if there is an expectation that a Head of I&D will come in to make change but they then find that they have a middle management role with little or no autonomy and limited access to leaders. Ideally the Head of I&D will be a catalyst and enabler, driving the I&D strategy and taking an advisory role within the organisation. Enable others to take accountability and help drive I&D through their own business strategy, which is when it starts to resonate.

You want to see the I&D topic everywhere. You want people to be talking and thinking about it during their working day, truly embedding it and role modelling I&D.

The I&D practitioner can either be an individual contributor creating executive sponsorship and allies throughout the organisation, or they can build their own team. For example, they may wish to build their team as shown in Figure 3.1. This provides resource to the Head of I&D, with roles and responsibilities in place. For example, an I&D Programme Manager may be responsible for I&D programmes, whereas the I&D Managers may be responsible for other areas that are in the I&D strategy. It is important to set clear objectives that complement each role in the team.

I&D practitioners are expected to make huge change – ask any practitioner the energy it takes to drive I&D. They will have strong influencing skills to enable them to really change people's views on I&D, educate them, and have an effect on people at all levels. They will have patience to get the topic on the agenda, bring people on the journey with them, go back to the starting block if there

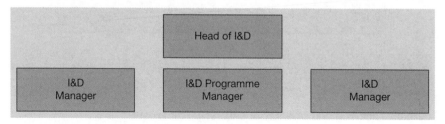

Figure 3.1 Example of an organisation chart

is little or no understanding of the topic, and at the same time they will be expected to create a culture of inclusion. This is where executive sponsorship can really help embed I&D into the organisation.

Executive sponsorship

Part of the structure is to build a portfolio of executive sponsors. A sponsor is someone who champions and supports I&D at a senior level. Sponsorship must start at the top.

Appointing executive sponsors is important. It needs careful consideration as to who that person might be as they will need to invest the time. It is a voluntary role in addition to their day job.

Executive sponsors need to operate across the different parts of the organisation and this depends on how the structure is made up. For example, you may consider a sponsor per operating team, division, country or central function (see Figure 3.2). As you select your sponsors, you want to ensure you have a diverse group spread across the organisation's footprint. You will need to have someone who sits on the board or leadership team and is willing to talk about it, challenge and support their peers. You can never have too many sponsors, as long as their role has clarity and is actionable. The larger and more complex the organisation, the more sponsors are recommended, to ensure each part is represented. In a smaller organisation, there may be fewer sponsors. A good mechanism is to calculate employee mass versus the percentage of executive

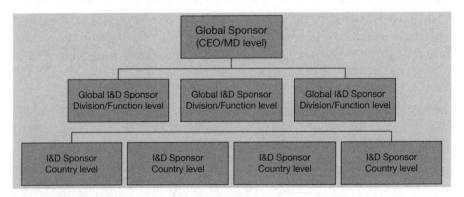

Figure 3.2 Inclusion and Diversity Sponsorship Framework

sponsorship across the organisation. You could calculate it based on numbers of boards/leadership teams your organisation has and where they operate.

Choose wisely: you may have a leader who wants to be a sponsor, but does not necessarily meet the role profile to undertake the voluntary tasks. The first question to ask a sponsor is: 'Why do you want to do it?'

Ask your sponsor: 'Why do you want to do it?'

When you have the answer, ask them the same question again. These sponsors are likely to be senior leaders and you will want to hold a form of interview with them, discuss why it is important to them and what they want to get out of it. Asking them 'why' is an important start to understand each other.

Interviewing a potential sponsor

It sounds formal, but as you set up your structure, it needs to be formal to gain the gravitas it requires. Below are sample questions you can ask a leader when appointing them as a sponsor:

- What is your understanding of both inclusion and diversity?
- Why do you think it is important to a business?
- How will you remove obstacles and barriers for I&D to be successful?
- What does respect and fairness look like to you?
- Do you see yourself as a role model? If so, give some examples.
- How would you regularly communicate I&D to employees and peers?
- Why do you want the role?

Also, look out for the following signs:

- What is the general reputation of this leader?
- Has this leader been linked to inappropriate behaviour, or a complaint?
- Is this leader prepared to be active given their demanding role?
- Is this leader prepared to challenge at their peer level and be educated on the topic, learn new things and be curious?

As you build a portfolio of sponsors, you want to ensure you have strong leaders in sponsorship roles who have a good reputation.

I remember a senior leader asking to be the executive sponsor for I&D. When I looked into their background, I realised they wanted to 'clean up' the reputation they had from past behaviours that were not appropriate. There is no right or wrong; just be aware.

Executive sponsor: role profile

It is always good to create a 'role profile' and discuss it with the sponsor so they are clear on what is expected of them. For example:

- Recognise that I&D are intrinsic to the success and performance of the organisation.
- Challenge and remove obstacles in mainstreaming I&D issues.
- Create a positive work environment, placing a high value on respect and fairness.
- Remove any barriers that may slow progress around I&D issues.
- Actively support efforts to make the work environment respective and inclusive.
- Regularly communicate the benefits of I&D and the organisation's successes.
- Regularly talk about I&D and make it part of everyday language, behaviour and approach.
- Become a role model informally and formally – treat others with dignity and respect.

The sponsor will also need to go through their own education journey and become familiar with the topic. All too often, leaders are asked to volunteer to become a sponsor and do not have the knowledge or necessarily the vocabulary. Support them with books, articles and other materials to ensure continuous learning.

Organisations should not simply opt for 'female board member sponsoring the women's group' or 'gay leader sponsoring the LGBT+ group'. There is no right or wrong; just be aware of who you are selecting and why. The selection must be taken seriously to have credibility and impact. Sponsors need to be held accountable and be aware of how I&D fits into their everyday life, ensuring it is not an 'add-on' or an extra thing to think about. It needs to be integrated into everything they do – they must make it part of their conversations and participate in the employee social media channels. This enables employees to see the authentic side of sponsors, learn more about them and their own personal journey. Senior leaders holding sponsorship positions will help give I&D the attention it requires.

Communication

It is important to keep the conversation going. Sponsors will need to:

- continuously find ways to have the conversation at every level
- be comfortable in talking about the topic, perhaps showing vulnerability
- get into discussions that might be uncomfortable at times
- be able to answer difficult questions
- empower their peers to call each other out to ensure fairness and respect
- update their leaders (and peers) on the direction of I&D and its progress.

I&D needs to be a commitment for everyone at the top, not just the sponsors. Topics to share with their peers may include:

- progress against targets
- a reminder of the strategic direction
- updates on initiatives.

Being visible

Sponsors need to be visible and accessible in order to promote leadership support to I&D. While this is important, there needs to be a clear path for sponsors to know that if there are difficult conversations that cannot be handled by them, there is a process in place to know where to direct this concern. Creating a process for them to pass it to the right part of the organisation will equip them. Leaders are not expected to know how to deal with every concern that they face; they will need support and coaching. Figure 3.3 shows a reporting channel for difficult conversations.

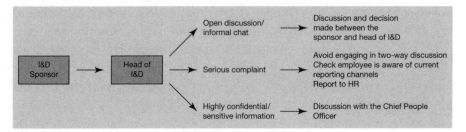

Figure 3.3 An example of a reporting channel for difficult conversations

I&D Councils

In addition to structuring an I&D team and identifying executive sponsors, you will need to set up I&D Councils. There are different ways you can structure I&D Councils depending on the organisation's structure and size.

What is an I&D Council?

An I&D Council is set up to help drive initiatives across the organisation and promote I&D. Typically, I&D Councils are made up of volunteers who help drive action and are part of a wider group that focuses on I&D. It is advisable to have an executive sponsor who is responsible for leading the I&D Council. I&D Councils need to become the powerhouse to drive action and can be set up to have:

- a diverse set of volunteers representing different areas of the business
- an I&D action plan
- an I&D communications plan to increase awareness and engagement
- a measurement tool in place that sets and monitors its goals.

Recruiting members to join an I&D Council

Once you have your executive sponsors, a fair and transparent process needs to be put in place so you can advertise to employees for them to apply to be a volunteer and sit on the Council, helping drive I&D. Firstly, criteria need to be put in place to help identify a diverse set of people at different job levels and titles to make up the Council. By selecting a diverse set of people, the Council will be able to have a far greater reach, hold more diverse conversations and interact with people who are outside their own teams. Everything you do must be inclusive!

It is important to give everyone in the organisation an opportunity to apply for a role on the I&D Council. Ensure:

- you select senior members as well as a representation at other levels, so everyone is considered
- there are criteria in place to help select members, and that those who are not selected are notified and encouraged to take part in different ways
- you harness the energy and embrace employees' desire to take part; the more employees there are building a movement, the more likely it is that change will occur.

Your chance to join the I&D Council

Our I&D executive sponsors are building their I&D Councils. We are looking for people who want to be part of building a respectful and fair environment across the organisation, have a voice and platform to share their views and be part of a change. These roles will be a commitment of one hour per month, plus some voluntary work to drive action in between the monthly Council meetings. If you are interested in applying for one of these roles, please write a 150–200 word document against the following criteria explaining:

- your motivation behind wanting to take part in the I&D Council
- your enthusiasm and commitment
- your ability to handle challenging discussions
- how you expect to change/develop as a member
- what you expect to gain from the experience
- your contributions to the Council
- knowledge you may have of I&D.

Suggested criteria for selecting members

When selecting members (the volunteers) to join the I&D Council, it is important to follow criteria that are fair and transparent. Below are suggested criteria.

Members of the I&D Council need to commit to:

- taking responsibility to help drive action

- acting as an I&D champion, identifying opportunities to ensure a fair and inclusive environment is enabled

- driving action through the organisation and demonstrating how it will help inspire a mindset shift for customers, clients and employees

- being aware of and supporting any network groups that are currently operating across the organisation

- taking part in monthly meetings. Member roles can be reviewed every 12 months, at the beginning of each financial year. If members are unable to attend three or more meetings in a year, they will have the opportunity to step down.

Selecting the members

Selecting members can be difficult, as they are all volunteering and supporting a good cause. However, it is important to recognise that members also need to have a good reputation in the organisation, not just the sponsors you choose. Like the sponsors, they will need to be a role model and have the ethical standards that are expected when leading I&D. From a performance point of view, you will want to check that they are not low performers, employees who are not performing in their role. This can be done by checking with your local HR team or their line manager, who also needs to approve the role.

Rotational places

You may wish to consider a couple of rotational places where these individuals have a seat at the table for 12 months and rotate off, taking their learnings back to their team. Thereafter two additional individuals are recruited to take their place. This enables the I&D Council to be mobilised and gives others the opportunity to take part.

Sub-working groups

Sub-working groups are a good idea if you are looking to focus on a specific topic, to go deeper into it and create further change. These specific topics should map back to two to three priorities set by the I&D Council keeping a strong focus on them. The sub-working group may be made up of other individuals in the organisation, led by an I&D Council member. This enables others to have the opportunity to get involved and be part of the action. The key is to have other I&D groups linked to the I&D Council, bringing it altogether under one approach so it gains momentum and is a stronger force without conflict.

Agree ways of working

Suggest meeting once a month, with sub-working groups working on initiatives in between the monthly meetings. Set no more than two to three priorities to focus on, reporting these priorities to the Head of I&D who will coordinate and report back to the organisation.

Agree terms of reference

It is important to lay out at the beginning as much structure as you can. Terms of reference will help build expectations, responsibility and clarity. For example:

- The sponsor is the decision maker of the I&D Council; all other members have an advisory and delivery role.
- The scope of decision making relates to I&D initiatives.
- All decisions made at the I&D Council must be legally compliant.
- The scope of the I&D Council includes all employees within the specific operating country.
- All current activities and initiatives that impact I&D are within the scope of the I&D Council.
- The I&D Council has the authority to stop, change or continue all such activities.
- Meetings will be held monthly. Each meeting will have minutes (attendees, actions, decisions) taken by a nominated member of the I&D Council and issued to the members to form the basis of review in the next meeting.

Create a local I&D plan of action

Once the members are in place (aim for approximately 8 to 12 members), the sponsor will lead the team into creating a local I&D plan of action that maps back to the global I&D strategy but is relevant to their local needs.

I&D Council action planning

A typical example of an I&D Council action plan can be seen in Figure 3.4. A clear plan is required where a purpose is identified. The purpose needs to be identified from up-to-date employee feedback. This can be from an employee engagement survey, focus groups or social media platforms. It is critical that the purpose of the I&D Council is diagnosed from feedback. The focus areas need to be created based on this feedback: the objective is to drive change in the areas where challenges have been identified. The feedback process must not be ignored, otherwise the areas of focus may not be addressing the challenges.

Create a communications plan

Nominate a communication lead on the I&D Council who is accountable in communicating the I&D plan, to increase awareness and engagement among employees across the country. Figure 3.5 is an example of a communications plan.

Reporting progress

Progress needs to be reported back to the Head of I&D, as well as challenges and barriers that are restricting any progress. The Head of I&D will need to hold regular meetings with their sponsors to advise and guide progress.

Measuring I&D Councils

It is important to measure progress and it is best to use an existing measurement tool within the organisation. You can find examples of KPIs in the earlier action plan (Figure 3.4). For example, if the organisation has an employee engagement

I&D COUNCIL – ACTION

I&D COUNCIL	PRIORITY #1	KPI	PRIORITY #2	KPI	PRIORITY #3	KPI
Business Area	**Women in Leadership** **1) Mentoring programme** **2) Development programme** **3) Senior women to take part in Board meetings**	x% representation at x senior level	**Generational Diversity** **1) Junior people to take part in Board meetings** **2) Reverse generational mentoring programme**	x% impact of mentoring – satisfaction scores	**Celebration Days:** **1) Pride month** **2) International Women's Day** **3) Mental Health Awareness Week**	x events x participants to raise awareness by y

Action Plan

WOMEN IN LEADERSHIP	GENERATIONAL I&D	CELEBRATION DAYS & ERGs
Mentoring programme – For women up to x job level – Identify mentors **Women in Leadership programme:** – For women at x job level **Board participation of women:** – Women invited to attend Board meeting	**Board participation of young people:** – x young people on x team to attend next board meeting	**LGBT+** – Employee resource group (ERG) in place – Plan Pride event **International Women's Day** – Plan event **Mental Health Awareness Week** – Plan event

Figure 3.4 An example of an I&D Council action plan

When	Core message	Audience	Vehicle	Writer / sender	Approvers	Deadline for review and approval	Send date to audience
Enter date	What is the core message?	Who are we talking to?	Email / social media channel	Name of person responsible for message	Communication team Sponsor Head of I&D	Enter date	Enter date

Figure 3.5   An example of a communications plan

survey and there are 'inclusion questions' inserted, extract these answers and measure the score year on year, or as regularly as you conduct the survey. Ideally you want to regularly monitor the scores three to four times per year.

Recognising I&D Council members

Remember I&D Council members are volunteers – think about rewarding and recognising them during the year. Invite them to annual conferences/events where they can network, share best practice and feel included in future strategy setting. After all they are taking this role because they are enthusiastic, passionate, knowledgeable and committed. At a central level, find ways that they can add their voluntary work into their own personal objectives, and support these conversations that they have with their line managers.

Keeping the momentum going

Be aware that there are many reasons why very little or nothing happens when setting a structure up around volunteers. These are great people with great intent to help improve the organisation, but it is important to be aware of the following points to avoid losing the momentum:

● The output of the session is overwhelming.

   ● Too many action points arise out of one meeting.

- No one has taken the time to consider following up.
  - Set follow-up times and hold each other to deadlines.
- No criteria were established from the outset.
  - Be very clear of expectations and who is accountable for what.
- No next steps are established at the end of the session.
  - Take from each meeting an outcome and who is responsible for what.
- The sponsor and/or Council members are not really committed.
  - Check in with energy levels and continued desire to commit.
- They are committed, but underestimate the effort required.
  - Be realistic about the amount of effort and time that needs to be assigned to the tasks in hand.
- The ideas are too threatening to key stakeholders.
  - Some ideas may be too ambitious for the organisation, so be realistic about the targets set.
- No one is accountable for results.
  - Be clear about who is accountable for what.
- The sponsor does not stay in contact with the volunteers outside of the regular meetings: 'out of sight, out of mind' takes over.
  - The sponsor needs to add to their calendar regular check-in times with the volunteers.
- The next meeting is scheduled to take place too soon.
  - Ensure you allow enough time for delivery, and come back to each meeting with updates.
- The output of the session is not documented.
  - Appoint someone in the group to take minutes and refer to these at the beginning of each meeting. This ensures people have followed through on their commitments. Rotate this role so it is fair.
- Volunteers' managers are not supportive of their time and effort.
  - A conversation must be had with the line manager to explain roles and responsibilities.

- Volunteers perceive follow-up as 'more work to do' instead of a great opportunity to make a difference.
  - This is not an add-on – it should be integrated into other tasks set as part of the day job.

With an I&D team, sponsors and Councils built firmly across the organisation, change can begin to take place. You can never have too many individuals when building a movement of change, so do not get too hung up on how many people you recruit. Go with the energy and ensure you have a collection of inclusive individuals who are going to help drive the cause in the right direction.

PART 2
HOW TO PUT THE I&D APPROACH INTO PRACTICE

CHAPTER 4
HOW TO EMBED I&D INTO THE BUSINESS STRATEGY

In this chapter we will discuss how to embed I&D into the organisation's strategies. There will be many different types of strategies across the business, and the aim is to have I&D in all of them. Whether that is the marketing, HR, business, behaviour or values strategy, it needs to be visible across them all. This enables employees, customers and other stakeholders to see that it is embedded and integrated into everyday practices.

Inclusion and diversity continues to be well researched and it is proven that focusing on it brings more diversity of thought into an organisation. Embedding the topic into as many strategies as possible will bring it to life. It is hoped that ultimately it will no longer be a debate and leaders will be open to embedding I&D into their approach to business. I&D must start at the top and be spoken about as part of an organisation's everyday strategic conversations.

By embedding it into leaders' mindsets and equipping them to think strategically about I&D, so they see it in the same light as any other business unit that has a strategy, targets and a measurement tool to track progress, you will help them to be accountable. They need to learn how to do this, and will need guidance around it. They don't know what they don't know.

Begin these discussions in as many areas as possible, such as:

- marketing
- customer/client relationships
- product development
- supplier relationships
- partner relationships
- sales

- design
- anything else that is critical in your end-to-end experience of what you do as an organisation.

If I&D is not visible, it will not be addressed.

Approaching different areas of the organisation

For example, meet with marketing and respectfully challenge their customer segmentation and target audience. For example, the Chief Marketing Officer should be having conversations around the customer-facing opportunities for diversity. How do they choose to inject diversity into their offerings – for example, what diverse markets are untapped or potentially ignored? Identify what is not being addressed. This information can be retrieved from existing channels such as customer satisfaction scores and feedback from your own diverse employees.

You may find blind spots and untapped markets you are excluding, because you simply have not thought about it in an inclusive and diverse way.

- What are you missing in your marketing?
  - Identify groups who are not present in your marketing.
- Who are you not talking or thinking about?
  - Identify groups that are not brought into the conversation.
- What and who might you not be considering?
  - Think of these groups and find ways to consider including them.

It is not just about the diversity of customers, it is also about their inclusion. Customers may visit your product or offering, but through looking at the feedback data, you can identify whether they experience inclusion.

Inclusion nudge

'Show the actual pictures of people used in company communications – internal and external'

Inclusive offerings

Designing in an inclusive way is only as good as the creator behind the design. If they have not experienced it, they will not know what individuals really want. For example, the fashion industry still uses terms such as 'nude' and 'naked' in reference to a pale skin colour. Plus-size garments are still modelled by non-plus-size models, so the clothes simply look baggy on them.

Technical language is still too complicated for the average customer to understand. Simplify language. For example, the mobile phone industry, rather than asking a customer 'How many megapixels do you need?' (quality of picture), simply ask 'What do you use your camera phone for?' This language is more inclusive for all customers.

Work with marketing/sales to increase understanding in the following areas:

- One customer does not fit all.
  - Customers receive the same message, but interpret them in different ways.
- Be aware of the benefits of having a diverse employee base who serve the customers.
  - They will be better able to serve the customer by understanding their needs better.
- Understand the customers' diverse needs.
  - Recognise the diverse needs of customers by asking diverse employees who experience the same needs.
- Use all-encompassing and inclusive language.
  - De-bias the language you use.
- If your sales force are on commission and have priority items, understand whether this is going to inhibit inclusion.
  - Do a checklist of what the priority items are, and audit the items based on how exclusive they may be.

Work with as many business units as possible and have a joined-up approach, with I&D underpinning your decisions at every stage (Figure 4.1).

As soon as I&D can be embedded into as many relevant areas as possible, accountability will begin to shift from the I&D function to the business leaders who are leading these areas in the organisation. If this is seen to be a commercial conversation, these leaders will be even more interested.

Depending on your offering, solutions and customer base, begin by thinking where the niche is. You could consider the following points:

- Spotlight the segment of the market that serves older women.
  - This could be where the higher disposable income is = opportunity for business.

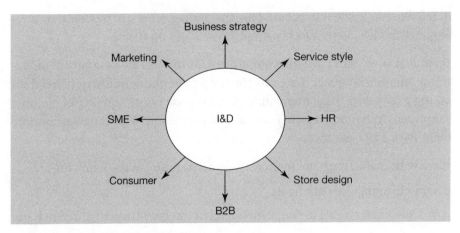

Figure 4.1 Embedding I&D into the business units

- Challenge who could become the next core customer.
  - Do not let past practices limit thinking or obscure your view of the opportunity ahead = opportunity for business.
- Specific groups want different approaches; for example,
  - Women
    - want to be connected with. . . not sold to
    - want to feel they are being understood and partnered with; they don't want to be fending off a sales pitch.
  - Disabled community
    - want inclusive access for customers who use a wheelchair
    - want an accessible user experience from finding an item online through to purchase.
  - Older customers
    - want intelligent advertising and real images.

By having the conversation with leaders in different areas of the business and explaining what is in it for them, you can help them understand commercially how I&D can bring benefits to their area. Leaders are very willing to change if they can see what this will do for them in terms of success.

Further resources

Nielsen, T. and Kepinski, L. (2016). *Inclusion Nudges Guidebook*, p. 40.

CHAPTER 5
WHY IT IS IMPORTANT TO SET TARGETS AND MEASURE SUCCESS

Every other business unit in an organisation sets targets. I&D as a business unit is the same. Target setting is crucial in order to measure progress. You want to set targets across as many interventions as you can, and put a measurement tool in place so you can track progress. The two go together:

- Set the target.
- Measure the progress.

Targets are different to quotas. There is often confusion about the difference between targets and quotas.

> **Targets** are aspirational goals that an organisation might set itself but not mandate.
> **Quotas** are mandated outcomes decided and announced by leadership.

In this chapter, I will discuss setting targets rather than quotas. Setting targets across as many different interventions as possible will better serve the organisation in driving I&D to a stronger position. These targets will be integrated into the review of processes, discussions and decisions on future planning, and I&D will be part of these critical planning points.

Below are a few examples of target setting across interventions that will integrate I&D into existing processes.

Recruitment

- **Graduate programmes**
    - Include diversity types from different cultures, academic backgrounds, ethnicity, and of different gender, for example 50 per cent male/50 per cent female.

- **Diverse interview panels**
  - Set a target for diverse interview panels: a mix of backgrounds. A diverse interview panel can be made just by using common sense. This is better than stipulating that we need to have one woman on the interview panel, this does not necessarily shift the needle. You can become unstuck with this method, as you will find yourself wondering: what do I do next, find a Black person, a gay person? Using a term such as 'a diverse interview panel' does not single individuals out. It brings a diverse group together, where everyone's views will be different, yet respected.

Development

Below are suggestions to ensure diversity is represented and invested in different parts of the development process. Data will always be a challenge, because of data points that cannot be captured, so work with what you have, then consider setting targets across the interventions listed below.

- **Promotions**
  - Track who you are (1) promoting, (2) developing and (3) offering stretch assignments to, against different diversity groups.
- **Succession plans**
  - Track who sits on (1) succession charts, (2) talent grids and (3) high potential lists, and identify the different diversity groups that are present.
- **Development programmes**
  - Look at who is selected for development programmes and at the accessibility of the programme to ensure it is inclusive to all. I remember a Head of Learning & Development who loved outdoor activities. They put a development course in place where participants had to go into the woods and build 'x' and then find their way back. It was not inclusive to everyone on the delegate list and some great talent stepped out of the development programme rather than put themselves through an experience they may have found very uncomfortable.

Retention

- **Leavers**
  - Track who is leaving and who is staying. Look at the diversity groups among these leavers.

- **Satisfaction**
  - Track who is satisfied and who is not. This can be achieved by slicing data in your employee survey (among those diversity groups that are captured). Identify where the employee satisfaction scores mostly sit and with which diversity group. This can be sliced by (1) job level and (2) job family.
- **Diversity pay gaps**
  - Set a target to close pay gaps among different diversity groups. Are you prepared to close the gap? How much will that cost? A Head of Talent Acquisition once said to me: 'If you want to solve this pay gap, give me the cash and I will solve it by Friday.'

By auditing as many interventions as possible through a process, you will be able to move barriers and free the process from bias.

Setting targets on the above interventions may seem bold for some organisations. There may be discussions around tokenism and positive discrimination. For example, some may think 'this just means we will promote or hire diversity to meet our targets'. Be ready to answer these questions. If an organisation is committed, it needs to stand by its commitment. Here is an example of a suitable response: 'Act in a positive way – "positive action" is different to "positive discrimination".' The following examples show the difference between positive action and positive discrimination:

'I will be more positive in my actions, by recognising and acting upon diversity' rather than 'I will promote or hire diversity to meet my target.' Positive action is an '**AND**'. . .

'I will be more positive in my actions, by recognising and acting upon diversity **AND** this person brings different experience and cultural knowledge to the organisation, complementing the current team's abilities etc.'

How brave is your organisation?

It is important to find this out first. By setting bold targets, change will occur more quickly. For example, an action plan behind a bold target may include the following:

Bold target: Increase senior female representation in the technology division.

- Focus on hiring senior women from the technology industry.
  - Incentivise them to join your organisation.

- Put an internal development programme in place so women from other areas of the business can move into technology, transferring their skillsets.
  - Introduce an internal mobility programme that develops transferrable skills
- Develop women lower down the organisation.
  - Positively take action to promote them into senior roles.

If the organisation commits to being bold in its approach to targets, then pro-active action planning like this needs to be put in place for the target to be met. By being less bold, progress might be slower, but the process may be fairer.

Whichever approach is taken, it needs to be agreed, and over what timeline – setting this is critical. Setting targets over timelines creates clarity and provides an action plan that will show the change over a period of time.

Setting targets across many touchpoints will raise awareness among the leaders, which will keep the process sustainable and present. Below is an example of setting a target.

Increase diverse representation at leadership levels

A common starting point for an organisation is to have more women in leadership positions, increasing female representation and, if it is male dominated, creating a more equal environment of women and men in decision-making roles.

Table 5.1 is an example template that could be used to set targets for greater female representation, but this model could also be used for other diversity groups. It shows two basic job levels ('senior 1' being the top and 'senior 2' the next job level down from the top). Ideally you should set targets at as many levels down from the top as possible, so you become aware of the current pipeline of female talent, understanding representation at each of these levels. Once the female representation becomes more balanced, for example, you may begin to identify this at 'job level 5'. This will be a critical point at which to undertake analysis on why women are not progressing their careers into more senior roles. This can be referred to as 'women hitting the glass ceiling'.

Table 5.1 An example template for use in setting targets for greater female representation

BUSINESS UNIT	CURRENT HEADCOUNT	JOB LEVEL: SENIOR 2		JOB LEVEL: SENIOR 1	
		Female Target	F/M (Actual)	Female Target	F/M (Actual)
COLUMN 1	COLUMN 2	COLUMN 3	COLUMN 4	COLUMN 5	COLUMN 6
MARKETING	153F/74M/11 Blank	–	8F/3M	+1	0F/3M
	64%F/31%M/5% Blank	–		= 33%	
FINANCE	758F/614M/99 Blank	+13	10F/31M	+5	4F/12M
	52%F/42%M/6% Blank	= 32%		= 31%	
HR	423F/106M/58 Blank	–	20F/6M	–	14F/2M
	72%F/18%M/10% Blank	–		–	
TECHNOLOGY	129F/595M/30 Blank	+1	0F/3M	+2	1F/8M
	17%F/79%M/4% Blank	= 33%		= 22%	
CUSTOMER	3909F/4379M/666 Blank	+29	19F/47M	+10	8F/15M
	44%F/49%M/7% Blank	= 44%		= 44%	

When you calculate

- **Column 1: Business Unit**
  - Ensure you have the full data: include every business unit that is listed in the database you are retrieving the data from.
- **Column 2: Current Headcount**
  - When retrieving the data, this becomes your baseline.
  - Date your baseline data.
  - Gather all the data; for example, you may have retrieved male and female data, but there may be other categories in the database, such as non-binary categories. In the above example, an extra category is 'blank'. This data shows individuals who are not categorised as male or female.
  - When collecting the current headcount data, ensure the decision is taken as to whether the data will include full time, part time, contract/freelance etc. By including part time, it will be more inclusive and encourage discussion around job sharing and part-time senior leader roles.

- **Column 3: Senior 2, Female Target**
  - Based on the current headcount, set a target that helps you achieve a more equal baseline of men and women, over the period of time you set (e.g. 12 months).
- **Column 4: Senior 2, Actual Numbers**
  - This column shows the actual numbers of male and female that are currently at this level.
- **Columns 5 and 6: Senior 1, Female Target and Actual Numbers**

  These columns show the top level (often referred to as the executive level, which sits one level down from the board).

Setting targets will depend on the function and its female representation. HR will be different to Technology. It may be found that in Technology the overall female representation is 20 per cent and in HR the overall female representation is 80 per cent. This is an example of needing to set targets unique to the business unit, increasing the percentage but not approaching this as a 50 per cent female/50 per cent male representation everywhere. If the overall female representation in Technology is 20 per cent from entry level to senior level, the focus becomes 'how to attract more women into the technology organisation', then look to push them up and through the pipeline over an agreed timescale so that you can create a more gender-balanced Technology department. Targets also need to be based on research from different industries. Researching externally to obtain a benchmark is a good start, then bring this into your own baseline. For example, the average representation percentage in Technology is 17 per cent in some countries, so look at your own baseline and then develop a realistic target over time that is achievable.

Organisations are data driven, and a huge challenge for the I&D function is that it struggles to retrieve accurate data, due to what is allowed to be collected (legally), or the systems which collect the data. Work with what you can get. Put caveats in and expect the leaders to help improve the systems that the data is being retrieved from.

Opting in is a good way to retrieve (at least) some form of data (depending on national laws). For example, you may want to retrieve data from a survey, so asking employees to opt in as much as possible will help. The caveat will be that the data retrieved will have a number of limitations, such as:

- the number of employees who are prepared to opt in and declare
- the response rate of the survey.

Do not get stuck in the data conversation – bring leaders out of that conversation. Remember this is where they are most comfortable, it is what they are used to and are ready to challenge. Get on a level footing and explain to them: 'We have to work with what we have, otherwise we will never move the conversation on'. If quantitative data is hard to collect, move to qualitative data, giving real-life employee examples, such as feedback from employees. This can be as valuable as quantitative data, but can be hard to prove when organisations are so data driven.

Have the end in mind: what you want to achieve when the data is retrieved and analysed. Keep it in mind that targets will enable the I&D function to track progress and measure success overall. This is where you want to get to:

- What does success look like?
  - I have obtained x data and am ready to activate my plan.
- How will you know when you get there?
  - I have identified the pain points and can confirm the diagnosis.
- What will the data look like when you get there?
  - 50 per cent complete/0 per cent complete/100 per cent complete.

By keeping the end in mind, you can begin to address the challenges and opportunities identified.

Linking targets to leader objectives

When setting a target, consider linking it to leader objectives that will have an impact on their financial reward, such as a bonus. Setting an I&D objective to leaders at a specific senior job level is a good way to keep the focus and commitment to I&D targets. For example, every leader is accountable for the gender diversity target that the organisation has set. Even if leaders are not directly hiring or promoting, they will be accountable to help achieve the target. They can do this through encouraging peers to attract, retain and develop more diversity, and talk about I&D frequently. Every leader needs to be accountable regardless of whether they can directly or indirectly impact the target.

Be clear on what will happen if the target is not reached. What will the impact be on their bonus, or what other consequence will there be of not achieving the target? This goes back to asking how bold your organisation wants to be when setting targets.

Measurement

If you haven't measured it, you can't manage it.

CHAPTER 6
WHY ORGANISATIONS TEND TO START WITH GENDER DIVERSITY

In this chapter we discuss why organisations have tended to start with gender diversity and putting support structures in place to achieve gender diversity goals.

Mainly it is because they can count the numbers of men and women, and organisations are data driven. This is not good enough – every aspect of diversity needs to be invested in, and organisations also need to invest in inclusion.

When we can see people for who they are, learn and better understand difference, we can begin to move the discussion on to seeing the intersectionality in people rather than seeing each other as if they belong to just one diversity group. Amy Bell (2018), in a special report for the *Financial Times* about intersectionality, states that we should 'look at the individual, not the minority group'. She goes on to say that 'we have had to push past looking at diversity in silos and really look at it from a human perspective'.

By learning more about each other, we create a learning environment that helps us better understand people's differences, regardless of their background. We have a long way to go, but this must be part of the end goal.

Gender diversity programmes

In the meantime, a common approach that organisations take is to create development programmes to help men and women better understand and navigate gender diversity. This is where many organisations start, and below are examples of how a programme can be designed. It is important to note that the programme designed can be relevant to other diversity groups, yet be mindful that the content may differ, based on your audit.

Women in Leadership programmes

Organisations invest in Women in Leadership programmes with the intent of developing female talent to progress through their talent pipeline in order to achieve a better gender balance in decision-making roles. If this type of programme is to be considered, it is important to set it up in such a way that the organisation's aim is to provide a better gender balance at senior levels, otherwise such programmes may be seen as 'fixing the women' rather than 'fixing the organisation'. The organisation, the system and its processes must be 'fixed', not the women.

Programmes for women should ideally be set up to provide a safe space, an environment in which women at a certain job level can discuss their careers with each other, as they may be regularly operating in a non-dominant group. At a certain job level the 'glass ceiling' may occur, where women are not moving through the pipeline, and data may show a drop-off in female talent at that level. The aim is to identify at which job level this is happening.

There is a range of programmes that are targeted to women and their careers. The first step is to diagnose the problem. For example, you may want to identify:

- Why are women hitting the glass ceiling and at which level?
  - When you have identified at which level they are hitting the glass ceiling, analyse what the problem is: you can run focus groups or individual interviews to obtain a greater understanding of what is happening. Be mindful to also hold the focus groups and individual interviews with men at this level to obtain a comparison, and a fuller picture of how men and women operate at this specific level.
- Why are women leaving and at which level?
  - Analyse the attrition rate and notice the increase at that job level. Look at any exit interviews, or reasons for leaving to find themes. Match this against how many men leave at the same job level and ensure you are weighting this to the number of roles held by men and women. Again, this will provide you with a better picture as to why both men and women are leaving. There could be a theme, such as a management issue, regardless of gender.
- What is the female representation on succession plans, high potential lists etc.?
  - Count the number of roles against men and women holding these roles, and then look at the succession plan to identify whether it will support the

gender balance you are looking to achieve. Mechanisms such as these need to be working to support the gender balance you are aiming to achieve.

- What is the distribution of performance ratings, pay increases etc.?
  - This data can then be compared with the data for men, This will give you insight into where the performance ratings are distributed, the bonuses and pay increases. You may find that women are receiving higher performance ratings than men, but men are receiving higher pay rises than women. Again, this mechanism needs to be working to support the gender balance you are looking to achieve, or in this instance, help close the gender pay gap.

Once these questions can be answered, and the diagnosis is done, you will be able to identify at which job level women are the least happy, or the most frustrated. The answer might be linked back to a higher attrition rate at this level, which will build on your theory about where the pain point is, or the 'glass ceiling'.

Targeting the women

At the identified job level is where you want to target the women for your programme, plus one job level lower. By targeting these two job levels, you will be able to hear from the women who are at the job level which states it is the toughest, and you will also be able to support the women at one job level below who are looking to move up into that job role.

Selecting the women

Women will be selected because they are high potential and talented, part of the organisation's future. Below are example criteria for selecting the participants:

- strong delivery and performance
- potential for future leadership
- high 'rating' and 'competency'
- documented as a high potential employee, potentially sitting on a succession chart.

The selected women

Once the women have been selected, there needs to be a questionnaire or equivalent to understand the barriers that women may be facing at the identified job level. By understanding the challenges women face in the organisation, the programme design can address it. For example, challenges may be:

- inflexible work practices
- working in a male-dominated environment
- access to stretch assignments
- visibility and networking
- juggling work and home life
- raising their personal brand
- self-limiting behaviours.

Once the barriers and challenges to progression have been identified, you can then build a development programme around them. Remember, this is not a stand-alone programme: the barriers and challenges that are discovered will also help the focus to change the processes and practices so that they can be removed, and the system can become more inclusive.

Notifying the selected women

Once the organisation is clear why the women have been selected, communicating the above points to the women themselves is important so that they understand they have been chosen on merit, not because they 'need' a programme.

Notifying the line manager

Make sure their line manager is notified, and that it is explained to them they play an important role in the success of the programme. Encourage them to have a conversation with the selected individual and discuss their strengths, development areas and personal expectations for the programme, aligning this with career performance and ambition. Also be clear with the selected women what their line manager will be looking for:

- How will you know that their attendance on the programme has been a good use of their time?
- How would you like them to apply the skills gained on the programme in their daily role?
- What can be done to provide further stretch in their role, to support their progression as a female leader? Be clear what 'progression' could look like, such as a bigger role, international experience, stretch assignment, promotion etc.

The objectives of the programme

First, objectives need to be set out for the women who are selected to attend the programme, both for them and for the organisation. Here are some examples.

For women attending the programme:

- Invest in them and increase their career prospects.
- Provide a confidential and supportive environment to explore their leadership.
- Tailor the programme to suit the multiple needs across the group, providing appropriate levels of stretch and challenge, making it relevant to their current situation.
- Support the development of the participants as they progress their career, providing a cohesive and rich learning opportunity.
- Encourage delegates to capture their learning and regularly reflect on the insights gained.

For the organisation endorsing the programme:

- Build a more skilled, differentiated and diverse global workforce.
- Support the continued evolution of the workforce.
- Support the programme, understand the business benefits and help drive the change that is needed, leading to a more balanced leadership in senior roles.
- Ensure women are progressing equally to men, and create the change that is required to build a gender-balanced organisation.
- Understand how to build inclusive leaders for the future, question how well the organisation is doing at retaining diverse talent and recognise more female role models.

The content can be made up around the barriers and challenges that women in the organisation face, and other factors. For example, these may be:

- the **environment** they work in
- the **aspirations/career goals** that women have
- the **values** and **identities** they hold
- their **behaviours** as they navigate their career
- the **capabilities** they have and how their self-belief allows them to prosper.

The advantages of a Women in Leadership programme

The investment in a Women in Leadership programme can be huge if the organisation supports it and it is set up correctly with the individuals. Communicating to the women who have been selected (and the women who have not been selected) is critical. It cannot be set up as though women need help, or as though it is an exclusive programme (the opposite to inclusive!). It needs to:

- be set up specifically to look at the development needs of women
- raise the awareness of challenges women face, when working in a non-dominant group
- address such challenges and build a future network of empowered women across the organisation.

Understanding the needs of the selected women

As you understand the needs of the participants, you can assess their current experiences. Below is a series of statements that could be used along with a scale of 1 to 10, with 1 being the lowest score and 10 being the highest.

I am clear about what I want to achieve in my career in the next 3–5 years

1	2	3	4	5	6	7	8	9	10

I feel that progression into a more senior role is an achievable goal for me

1	2	3	4	5	6	7	8	9	10

I have at least one senior mentor who is actively supporting my career development

1	2	3	4	5	6	7	8	9	10

I have a network of strong working relationships across the organisation that will help me to further my career

1	2	3	4	5	6	7	8	9	10

I understand the common barriers that can impede women's success in the workplace and have strategies to overcome these

1	2	3	4	5	6	7	8	9	10

I have practical tools to enable me to reflect on and challenge the way I lead

1	2	3	4	5	6	7	8	9	10

I am confident I have the skills and abilities to achieve my goals

1	2	3	4	5	6	7	8	9	10

I understand my leadership strengths and development needs

1	2	3	4	5	6	7	8	9	10

I feel confident about my personal impact

1	2	3	4	5	6	7	8	9	10

I have a personal career plan

1	2	3	4	5	6	7	8	9	10

Engaging the organisation as well as women

Gender diversity needs to be addressed as part of the business/HR strategy. This highlights that it is the organisation (not the women) that needs to move: From (identifying the challenges) . . . To (removing the challenges). . . . Table 6.1 gives some typical findings that may be considered.

Table 6.1 A template to help identify and remove the challenges that women face

From	To
Lack of access to influential networks	Be visible to those in positions of influence with the potential of being considered for roles as they become available
Little or no focus to address the gender gap in the organisation	Support great women who have potential
Lack of sponsorship for bringing more women into senior positions	Identify sponsors in leadership who take an active interest in women's career development and ensure they are known by others in the organisation, giving women stretch assignments to help build their experience and profile
Lack of female role models, emulating only specific types of potentially non-inclusive behaviours that both men and women adopt	Give women access to female role models, building a network of empowered women who themselves will become role models/mentors for the next generation of women, paying forward their experiences to other future talented women
Women holding back from putting themselves forward for senior roles, doubting their ability to take on senior-level tasks and roles	Enable women to become more conscious and help them navigate through the 'organisational labyrinth', addressing the challenges of organisational politics and performing certain tasks and roles adequately
Lack of self-awareness	Enable women to gain deeper insights and self-awareness on their performance and behaviour from their team/line manager/peers/senior managers
Lack of network support	Enable women to work in group activities, giving them the chance to develop and learn together as a group. Share experiences and specific challenges they face as women in the organisation

I remember delivering a Women in Leadership programme, where I asked the participants to:

> Stand up if you have been up for promotion in the last three years.
>
> Stay standing if you are hungry for promotion.

Three out of 40 women stayed standing, and in that moment I realised that women did not want the promotions. This became the core of the conversation: why promotion was not attractive to them. Some example responses were:

- I do not want to be part of a male egotistic environment.
- I do not want to travel the world like the leadership team does.
- I do not want to work 24/7 like they do.

This type of conversation then begins to define the culture of the leadership team and determines whether it is even an attractive place to work for women. These findings will likely be similar for other individuals from non-dominant groups.

Measuring the success of the programme

In order to ensure the programme is a success, you want to regularly monitor it, preferably every quarter/six months. Calculating the percentage of one or more of the following will enable you to track the programme's success:

- performance increase among participants
- salary increase among participants
- turnover (voluntary and involuntary) among participants
- promotions/stretch or international assignment.

Risks linked to the programme

There is a risk that the programme will be perceived negatively by others if it is not communicated and managed well. Look out for the following negative perceptions:

- It is about 'fixing the women'.
- The women feel like a victim being 'sent to a diversity programme'.

Ensure the programme is a leadership and development programme that is part of the leadership and development strategy to help women navigate their career and that it maps back to the organisation's business strategy, which clarifies the criticality of needing more diversity at the top. The women need to be assured that they are on the programme because they are classed as high potential and that while the programme is in place it will also be part of an effort to ensure the organisation is addressing the removal of any barriers or challenges they may face as a result of its commitment to a more gender-balanced organisation.

Men-only diversity programmes

A Chief Human Resource Officer (CHRO) once said to me: 'If I gave you one budget to use on one programme, would you use that to invest in women or invest in men in the gender diversity discussion?'

This made me think very differently. At one point in my career, in partnership with Tyche Consulting, I designed a 'men-only diversity programme'. The aim was to equip and upskill male leaders (in this case they were the dominant group) in the I&D discussion. Men are not engaged in the debate enough, and there are comments made, labels used, that is, it isn't the men in the room making these comments. It is others outside the room 'pointing the finger' which does not help, such as 'white middle-aged men' and 'white men at the top'. These are unhelpful and all they do is push male leaders further into a corner.

We need to move towards including everyone in the discussion, engaging everyone in the topic and moving away from 'women talking to women about women'. Otherwise a potential downside to diversity programmes is that they can create a 'them and us' and segregation of groups. This segregation can sometimes lead to groups becoming divisive and exclusive, the opposite to inclusive.

A 'men-only' diversity programme can be controversial, and even more so if it is mandated. Yet this type of programme must start at the top, where generally there may be more male leaders. It is a bold move that goes back to the question: how bold does your organisation want to be in its I&D efforts?

Being bold and putting a men-only diversity programme in place helps male leaders be more included in the I&D discussion. Sometimes they are excluded and usually talked about, which becomes a bigger problem. When they are excluded from the discussion they will learn less and have limited vocabulary, watching every word they say, believing they will be scrutinised, and ending up not saying anything at all on the topic. They may be afraid to connect with people who are different to them, because of what might be said.

Male leaders need an environment that is set up to safely hold the discussions that may feel uncomfortable. The aim is to bring the discussions and questions out in the open and understand what it all means to them. When a safe environment is created, conversations can be brought to the table and approaches can be discussed. Questions will vary because male leaders will be at different parts of their own I&D journey.

Communications are critical when setting up a men-only diversity programme. Employees and the delegates need to be aware of how it fits into the organisation's strategic thinking and approach. The programme needs to be linked to why it makes business sense to run it, and delegates need to be clear what the business rationale is behind the programme. They need to understand why they are attending. Below are examples of goals that could be communicated:

- Become **fully inclusive** in the way we think and behave.
- Become more **aware**, begin to **care**, and **dare** to be different about inclusion.
- **Learn and unlearn** and open our mindset; probe our own thinking.
- Broaden our vocabulary so we can better understand and engage in the I&D topic.
- Understand the **implications as leaders** if we stay the same.
- Understand why this makes **business sense** and how it connects to **performance and profitability**.

Creating a safe space for male leaders to ask a variety of questions they may not have discussed before is important, because the richer the conversation, the better their understanding will be of the topic. Some questions might be controversial or awkward, but the important thing is to get them out on the table and simply have the conversation.

The conversation might look like this:

- I see that we have affinity groups, Employee Resource Groups and networks. Can I join even if I am not representative of the group?
  - Yes! Be an ally. Allies are so important especially when leaders become one – it is a powerful signal to employees in the organisation that leaders are getting involved.
- Is women getting the top jobs a priority just to hit a target?

- No! Women are talented, and bringing them into decision-making roles will help the organisation to see things in a different way and bring a different perspective to the table. Women are promoted because they are talented, not because there is a target in place.

- How do I get rid of a poor performer who is in a non-dominant group?

  - The organisation should have a reliable and robust performance structure in place. By following this, you remove any thinking about the diversity of the individual. *However,* it is harder for employees who are from non-dominant groups, because they relentlessly navigate around dominant groups. It uses a lot of their energy up and they may be on the end of subtle unhelpful comments. Ensure you have a supportive ongoing conversation with those who find themselves in non-dominant groups before their performance is judged. It is not fair to go straight to the conclusion that someone is not performing without having these support conversations first. It is simply about looking out for the wellbeing of others.

    I particularly love the metaphor of the elephant and mouse that Laura Liswood discusses in her book *The Loudest Duck* (2010), one of my favourite books. In fact, I have bought this book for every leader I have ever worked with.

    The Elephant and Mouse story: 'The basic idea is that if you are the elephant in the room, what do you need to know about the mouse? Not much, for you are mighty, tall, and powerful, and have little use for the tiny creature. If you are the mouse in the room, what do you need to know about the elephant? Everything. You could be crushed or obliterated if you don't understand the elephant's habits, movements and preferences. The elephant knows almost nothing about the mouse, but the mouse survives by knowing everything about the elephant.'

    Here is the dynamic between the dominant and non-dominant. In this metaphor, the mouse represents the non-dominant, whose diverse and valuable skillsets, such as adaptability, flexibility, care with language, attention to detail, have been built over time from navigating their way through dominant groups.

    How can we really understand these dynamics of dominant and non-dominant groups, the subtle actions, unwritten rules, unconscious perceptions?

- Why do we need diversity – we are performing well and hitting our numbers?

- You do need diversity! Imagine how much better you would perform and operate if you brought more diversity of thinking to your organisation. It makes business sense to continue to bring in this diversity of thinking to become even more innovative and creative, leading the organisation to have a greater competitive edge.

During these conversations, it is important that the delegates understand it is not about giving right or wrong answers – it is about becoming aware of I&D. There is no silver bullet, but just to get the conversation going is an important step. This cannot be underestimated. It will feel empowering and liberating when these conversations happen.

What do you think? The answers to the above questions can be varied and in the programme it is important to ask the delegates: 'What do you think?' Facilitate the conversation so that they come up with the answers themselves.

The conversation is at the heart of better understanding and becoming more conscious of their own behaviour and how inclusive they are of different things.

There are also male leaders who might shy away from putting their hand up and getting involved in I&D activities, as they might be unsure about how their own career path will be perceived. We simply need to engage the men in the discussion, provide a safe space to help them better understand how they show up as a leader to others and embrace other viewpoints, recognising that they are part of the conversation.

I have been asked, 'How about bringing men and women together to have this debate?' Yes. But first, hold these conversations separately so the safe space is created, and no one feels threatened in this topical debate.

At the end of the programme leaders should be better equipped to:

- know what their 'elevator pitch' is for I&D
- hold each other accountable
- ask their own leaders or direct reports about diversity
- understand their role as leaders in the I&D topic
- pay it forward: share their learnings.

Whether the group is male or female, or a mixed group, getting the conversation on the table has to be the start. Many organisations go straight into 'training' without acknowledging the difficulty people have by just having the conversation. We are dealing with a very sensitive topic with different beliefs and behaviours working in systems. Have the conversation first before doing anything else.

Here is a quote from a men-only diversity programme:

> **'I gained a lot from the male-only workshop and the perspectives you have shared have truly left a lasting impression on me. I have become more conscious, have become more inclusive in my thinking and behaviour.'**

Sadly, though, whatever efforts organisations are making, it is still not enough. McKinsey & Co. (2020) reported that female representation on executive teams moved up just one percentage point from 14 per cent in 2017 to 15 per cent in 2019.

Further resources

Financial Times (2017). 'Female leaders boost the bottom line', Sarah Gordon, 27 September.

Financial Times (2018). 'Modern workplace', Amy Bell, 31 May.

Liswood, L. (2010). *The Loudest Duck.* NJ: John Wiley & Sons, p. 31.

McKinsey & Co. (2020). 'Diversity wins: How inclusion matters', May, p. 4. https://ucon.secure.nonprofitsoapbox.com/storage/diversity-wins-how-inclusion-matters-vf-2020.pdf

CHAPTER 7
THE VALUE OF DIFFERENT DIVERSITY GROUPS

Across any organisation, employees will belong to different diversity groups. Until we move the discussion on to talking about intersectionality – recognising that people belong to a variety of diversity groups – organisations will still tend to see individuals as being in one particular diversity group. Networks are formed and this increases the segregation of employees. However, networks are of real value to an organisation. They can have a real positive business impact on different areas, such as recruitment, retention, marketing to customers, product development and community outreach programmes.

For example,

- Learn to keep terminology simple, and be ready to evolve it over time, so vocabulary is broadened.
- Be inclusive and ensure the community is represented in policies, healthcare, pensions etc.
- Run an audit to identify whether the language used is inclusive, in areas ranging from recruitment, facilities, marketing materials and company website.

For example, help the organisation be inclusive of gender pronouns and encourage the use of them, so individuals are able to articulate which words they would like others to use when talking to or about them. The most commonly used pronouns are 'he, him, his' and 'she, her, hers'. The millennials are a generation that tend to no longer see gender as a fixed binary (e.g. just male or female). This view will grow even more when generation Z join the workforce in the mid-2020s.

Role modelling different diversity groups

Having role models is so important. If employees do not see a representation of themselves, especially in leadership positions, they may not be motivated to progress their career. They may believe that if the diversity group they belong to is not represented, then they will not be able to achieve a leadership position themselves.

Role models are beacons to other people who may be hiding their sexuality, disability, religion etc. Role models can be figureheads, they can be powerful and credible, demonstrating to others that it is possible to be yourself at work.

Allies who support diversity groups in which they are not represented

Allies are hugely important. They can be colleagues from different parts of the organisation who are supporters of a particular group they do not belong to. This helps build momentum and better understanding among employees. Being an ally can demonstrate that:

● you are willing to show action that may involve pointing out that a comment or joke may not be appropriate, thus standing up for your group

● you are willing to become a mentor to someone from an underrepresented group

● you apply your diversity lens to everything you do on a daily basis and encourage others to do the same; you are an advocate

● although you may not have lived the experience, by being part of the group you are willing to listen and learn how others are feeling and what they are experiencing

● you may be able to provide opportunities that are easier for you to reach than others, helping make the environment around you more equitable and fair.

Before you can feel empowered, you need to feel supported and understood

How allies can empower others: sometimes before you can feel empowered, you need to feel supported and understood.

This is where an ally can be really helpful. When you can become a true ally, you begin to empower others by taking action. *Act* by:

- supporting an individual's journey
- reaching out to them
- understanding them
- removing any barriers they may experience that you may not
- listening with intent and curiosity and checking in with them
- showing them they are valued, they are important, you heard them, their message got through
- being an informal listener, friend and public supporter
- being proactive, not passive (it is not 'just about wearing lanyards'), actively taking on the issues at hand.

Executive sponsor who supports different diversity groups

Identifying an executive sponsor is important, someone who is high up in the organisation who can help sponsor the cause. This leader can:

- Help educate other leaders to learn about I&D
  - They could talk about their own experiences of being part of a diversity group.
- Help raise awareness of any barriers and challenges that non-dominant groups have in the organisation
  - The sponsor may not experience the barriers that others might. By helping to remove them the sponsor can build a more inclusive environment.
- Grow the reputation of the diversity group
  - The sponsor could regularly talk about the group and their involvement.

Choosing the executive sponsor is important: just because a leader has put their hand up, it does not mean they are able to fulfil the role. See the selection as a formal process. For example:

- The group meets with the leader and initiates a conversation.

● Both parties agree to and understand their responsibilities.

● Share the ideas and plans to seek feedback from the executive sponsor, to better understand where they can add value.

Celebrating different diversity groups

Holding a range of celebrations to recognise different diversity groups is a good way to enable everyone to learn more about the particular group. For example, the organisation could have a Pride day to coincide with an event led by the LGBT+ community, many of which are held in June or July, depending on the nation.

It is not down to the I&D practitioner to put on as many celebration days as possible to show that the organisation is inclusive. Ideally with celebration days, the organisation wants to create a groundswell of activity encouraged by the employees. It is likely to be employees from different diversity groups that feel passionate about a specific cause. The role of the organisation is to empower and support them, providing a budget if required.

Things to be mindful of:

● Show balance – if you celebrate International Women's Day, you may want to celebrate International Men's Day too.

● If there is criticism that the organisation is not celebrating a specific day, encourage the critics to get involved and help organise.

● A topic may be chosen and it may not have any form of representation and be of no interest to the employees. Choose wisely.

● We are in this together – if there is something important to the employees, let them celebrate with the support of the organisation.

Employee Resource Groups (ERGs)

An ERG (Employee Resource Group), also known as a Network or Affinity Group, is a group that is created by employees and aims to address the needs and challenges of the diversity group that it represents. An ERG can create a safe environment for employees who share a common purpose and interest, helping them to feel they belong. It provides them with a safe space to discuss challenges and opportunities in the workplace.

In a *Financial Times* (2020a) special report on 'Diversity Leaders', Janina Conboye stated: 'Beyond initial goals to address workplace inequality and provide a safe space for sharing ideas, the focus is shifting towards how these ERGs can be used to help businesses evolve. Indeed, research published by Accenture, the consultancy, suggests that if all UK companies improved inclusivity by 10 per cent, the resulting innovation could increase GDP by up to 1.5% each year.'

These groups can bring rich diversity of thought to business challenges, increase retention rates and make the organisation look more attractive to potential employees and clients. These groups bring great benefits to any organisation.

- Recruiters can tap into their niche talent network to attract diversity.
- Anyone, at any level, can approach the group to gain knowledge and understanding.
- It enables employees to experience inclusion and belonging.
- These groups are cross-functional by nature, and they have knowledge about different markets and themes, due to their cultural awareness.

I discussed ERGs with Vusa Tebe, an I&D consultant. Vusa set up a BAME (Black, Asian and minority ethnic) ERG and describes the process.

Vikki: *Vusa, you set up a BAME ERG when you worked for a corporate organisation in the city – can you tell me how you went about starting one?*

Vusa: *It took a while for me to get there, but I went for it and just started one. When I first co-founded the ERG I had no idea what I was doing. All I knew was I wanted to create a space where BAME colleagues would feel seen, heard and most importantly understood. What that space looked like or how I would create it was still a mystery. But the biggest question I had was: would anyone even want to join?*

When we started our ERG my company at the time already had ERGs for LGBTQ+, Women in Leadership and the highly subscribed Pet Lovers so we didn't feel like we had to ask for permission to start one. But if you are in an organisation that doesn't have any established ERGs my advice is just do it!! Worry about permission later. What you are trying to do is bring people together for the good of the organisation and no self-respecting leader or organisation should have a problem with that. So, on a gloomy September afternoon my co-founder and I spent a lunch break creating an ERG on the company's social media platform and this was the beginning of an exciting, overwhelming and growth-filled journey.

We chose a name for the ERG, but what now?

The first thing we set about doing was raising the profile and letting people know we existed. We did this by hosting events to celebrate key dates for the community we represented. For us this included Black History Month, Eid, Chinese New Year and Diwali. We used these not only to entertain but to educate on the history and significance of those occasions. These events gave us an opportunity to bring in people from outside the organisation to talk about their experiences. For Black History Month, we hosted a panel discussion made up of senior-level Black professionals from various industries. What really hit me from that event was the similarities of experiences – while it was sad to know that systematic racism and micro aggressions affected all of us there was something comforting in knowing that I was not the only one having those experiences. This event also highlighted to me the importance of representation and visibility. It was the first ever panel made up of Black people the company had ever hosted and I did not know how truly impactful that would be. The amount of positive feedback from our colleagues was overwhelming and reinforced the importance of visibility, and that formed a big part of the ERG strategy we began to build.

We were determined to raise the profile of our BAME colleagues, and these events gave people a chance to speak not only about the cultural event but about how their culture influences them in different aspects of their life. This served as a great way to hear from our community about how they were feeling and to get conversations on the table. There is no one right way to launch an ERG as every company is different and has different needs. The most important thing is that you start something.

More than fun and games

When I first entered the world of ERGs, I initially thought maybe we would just be hosting a few events throughout the year. But I quickly realised that ERGs are so much more than Hong Baos and pitchers of rum punch. ERGs have the power to influence policies and processes that directly impact the community that they represent.

Vikki: *How do you get from parties to pushing for more inclusive processes?*

Vusa: *The first thing you need to do is start thinking of it as a department or function within the business. Therefore, like any department or function it should have a Vision, Mission and Purpose. As ERGs are often run by employees of the non-dominant group, members tend to be more junior employees so may not have experience in setting up a department or function.*

When starting an ERG the first thing to think of is: what is the purpose of the group and what does it exist to do? There is no right answer for this, and it will depend on where in the journey of diversity the business is and the specific challenges experienced by the non-dominant group it represents.

Purpose: Why will the group exist?

– Raise awareness.

– Provide a safe space.

– Promote the advancement of its members.

Vision: What is your ultimate goal?

– Make a difference to the lives of its members or the business.

Mission: This is the 'How'. What processes, policies and cultural shifts will you make to achieve your vision?

– Make people feel excited and part of a strong ambition or aim.

Values: These are the principles and values that will accelerate your progress together.

– Create a statement that typically starts with a verb, such as: 'Be committed' or 'Deliver excellence'.

– Write it in the company's voice.

Think about it like getting into a car – where are you going and why? I am going to the shop to buy milk because I like my coffee with milk. That is my purpose.

When I get the milk, my coffee is going to taste delicious and when I drink it in my lounge snuggled on the couch I will be instantly revitalised by the delicious nectar. I am then going to be ready to take on the day and its challenges. That is my vision.

How am I going to get there? I am going to get in the car, sing along to the song on the radio, follow the sat nav, park and go into the shop (with my mask for COVID). That is my mission.

Setting out your vision, mission and purpose makes it easier for you and everyone on the journey with you to stay on track. It also makes it easier to start identifying meaningful ways to measure your success. This is where identifying an executive sponsor can really help.

What is an executive sponsor?

An executive sponsor is a senior member (senior/executive leader) who will work with the group to help them navigate the business landscape and act as a sponsor for them in the rooms where they are not (yet). The sponsor can also act as a valuable sounding board and ask the hard questions to ensure plans are robust. I found having a sponsor the most helpful when we were trying to get budget. As ERGs tend to be set up by more junior employees, it is unlikely they will have experience of navigating the winding and rocky waters of securing budget such as

– Who do you go to?

– What questions will they ask?

– How much should you ask for?

– How do you spend it?

This is where having a sponsor is extremely useful as they can guide you and point you in the right direction. The key things to consider when choosing a sponsor are:

– What access do they have?

– Are they a decision maker or do they have direct access to the decision makers?

– How much time can they give you?

– How aligned to the cause are they?

There is no point having a sponsor that is connected but does not have the time, or is not part of decision-making processes. They do not necessarily need to be from the non-dominant group that the ERG represents, but you want to have a sponsor that is a true ally to really be an advocate for the ERG and act as a role model.

Do not be afraid to ask your sponsor these questions as they play a vital role and it is only fair that you lay out the expectations upfront.

Vikki: *Thank you, Vusa. Finally, what was your biggest learning and how did you personally develop through your experience of setting up the BAME ERG?*

Vusa: *What I learnt is that the voices of the non-dominant groups are not heard in the corporate world and the damage that this has caused is deeper than I first imagined. But as harrowing as some of the stories I have heard are, there is also no one better placed to make the changes necessary to the system than the groups affected. But getting organisations to the point that they recognise that is not always easy.*

Because the non-dominant groups are living with the everyday impact of systemic racism, they are the groups that can identify the best solutions to combat the problem, providing organisations are committed to making meaningful change and accepting accountability.

My time spent in an ERG has changed me massively – not only did I get to experience creating something from nothing, I got to see the impact it had on others to have a safe space in an organisation that represents them. When you experience having an organisation really listen to what you say and take on board and implement your suggestions, it changes how you feel about work as a whole. For me it opened my eyes to the possibilities and I made the choice to shift my career to focus on inclusion and diversity. I made that choice because I know I am not the only person to have experienced exclusion in the workplace and I am determined that people who come after me do not have those experiences. If I can support organisations on their journey to inclusion then that is exactly what I am going to do because the impact of that is huge.

Vikki: *Thank you for your wisdom here, Vusa.*

Vusa alludes to how she developed as a person, working tirelessly for her diversity group. Organisations should find ways to recognise these individuals. People who invest time in running diversity groups do the role over and above their day job. By putting a recognition plan in place, you will motivate them to continue in their great efforts. For example:

- Provide them with a gift voucher or an award to recognise their efforts.
- Add their efforts into their personal development plan.
- Incorporate their work into their objectives, making a percentage of their working time a contribution to their efforts. Twenty per cent is typically one day per week of a full-time working week. This can be a sensible approach.

For these individuals, the skillsets gained can be beneficial to their day job, and for the organisation this can go a long way to helping retain and develop talent. Participants may see the role as aiding career progression, linking it to their own performance and objectives with a view to what they want to achieve in the future. This is a neat way for organisations to develop their employees in a different and meaningful way.

Accessibility is also a broad topic that is not discussed enough. When I discussed disability with Caroline Casey, Founder of The Valuable 500, she talked about how broad the topic is and how to get it on the agenda.

Vikki: *Caroline, you are an advocate for disability, and an entrepreneur yourself. The Valuable 500 you founded is a mission to get disability on the business leadership agenda with organisations. Where are leaders right now in the discussion for disability?*

Caroline: *We've come a long way but we are not there yet. Disability business inclusion is still left on the sidelines compared to other topics, even though 72 per cent of families experience disability in some shape or form. Those living with a disability are still often seen as a 'damaged and not valuable'. We have to change this stigma and outdated perception so business sees the real value of this 1.3 billion people with a disability as customers, employees and members of the community. Governments and regulations still focus on employment of people with disabilities – but without educating organisations into the value this can bring, and encouraging them to share learnings, we will never make progress. Sustainable action will only come if and when CEOs (Chief Executive Officers) and leadership teams see and believe the value it brings, and the best way to address all of this is when learning takes place, learning from each other.*

The old saying 'he who shouts loudest gets heard' comes into play. According to business, 'the disability community is not angry enough'. I have heard organisations say, 'we need to respond to the louder voices', hence the focus on gender and race. But what we need is to stop pitting humanity against itself and argue for inclusion for all rather than maintaining a silo-based approach. It is no longer acceptable for business to wait and purely address the loudest issue – to be sustainable in the medium and long term they need to embrace inclusion for all.

Leadership from the top down is key – this should not be left purely to the CHRO (Chief Human Resource Officer) or CDO (Chief Diversity Officer). Metrics need to be in place. What gets measured gets done. If disability inclusion is absent in the metrics, nothing will happen and organisations will miss out on recruiting the best talent and serving a market worth $8 trillion pa.

Vikki: *You just talked about the customer. What types of experiences do people with a disability have when shopping, and online shopping more so since COVID?*

Caroline: *We imagine one size fits all; we imagine everyone has the same experiences. But what might work for someone might not work for someone else. As a visually impaired person, and as a consumer, it is incredibly difficult for me. The way most websites front ends are designed, how many clicks it takes, how accessible they are etc. turns customers away.*

And even in the current climate with the global pandemic, online tools such as Zoom and websites are often still limited in the correct tools they offer to be accessible. AccessiBe, an accessible technology company, recently tested 10,000,000 websites, the vast majority hosted in North America, for accessibility compliance. It found that 98 per cent of menus and 71 per cent of online forms failed – this is 'the walk away pound'.

For people with a disability this is discriminatory, and the lack of empowerment, frustration and forced dependence on others leads to anger. When things work online, for me it is joyful, it is like winning the lottery! It is a sense of joy. Amazon is making it ridiculously easy for me – the information is stored in my system, I do not have to enter numbers etc. which is hard for me. I will keep going back to the places I know and love.

Vikki: *We have seen movements and crises, such as Black Lives Matter, #metoo campaign, COVID forcing remote working for many. What are your views on movements?*

Caroline: *The tragic death of George Floyd and the Black Lives Matter movement; the clear inequity between genders; the issues associated with sexuality and the marginalisation of those people with a disability all need addressing. As I said, business tends to focus on the movements with the loudest voices. We need to shift the mindset of business and to truly see this from the point of 'intersectionality'. We do not fit into one box. I am a white woman, I have a disability, which box do I fit into? Each of our identities is made up of a whole range of factors – we are not defined by any one characteristic.*

Vikki: *How can we educate and equip leaders on the topic?*

Caroline: *Leaders need to take responsibility and accountability – leading from the front. We are in a decade of disruption, and we set up The Valuable 500 for CEOs and brands to learn from each other and reset the business system with regard to inclusion of people with disabilities across the entire value chain. The uncomfortable truth is that disability is complex and growing as the population ages. We will all know a close friend or family member that faces a disability at some point. Eighty per cent of disabilities are acquired between the ages of 18 and 64 and 80 per cent of disabilities are invisible.*

Many employees still hide their disability for the fear of being treated differently. In fact, EY did some research and identified that four out of five leaders are not declaring their disability. The trends are changing but too slowly and this needs a massive shake-up.

We know that leaders follow leaders and if we can create a place to innovate and sometimes fail, but give permission and understand the intent, we will do more. We cannot just stay in the place where 'we are not doing enough so we will not do anything'. The Valuable 500 leaders are leading the way.

Start by looking at 'who and what do we have now' – this is the great reveal! Simply go to the community and ask. It is ok to ask.

Ultimately, we need to get the voices heard from the disability community; those employees who already have a disability but currently hide it, find ways for employees to anonymously have the opportunity to share their situation and talk about their experiences. It would be great if all the CEOs who have signed up to The Valuable 500 ran an anonymous survey – imagine if we revealed a true number! Get it out of the closet and recognise that you already have disability in the workplace; you are already recruiting, retaining and developing great talent who may have a disability. It is about the great reveal!

We need to create a culture of inclusion for employees to come forward and begin an education process for everyone. Once this is done, you can then look to the disability community and ask for their advice, such as reviewing simple processes, language, job design, products and services. You can then identify what you are currently excluding.

Sharing best practice on disability needs to happen more. There are many I&D practitioners who are doing great work on disability, but it is not being shared enough. By sharing these ideas, we can scale good ideas. There are great examples that are not being scaled and therefore are not at the highest level. . . thus not attracting the investment they require. Let us just take language: it really annoys me that the new buzzword is 'differently abled', it is offensive. This encourages 'ableism', which just discriminates against those with a disability.

Vikki: *We talk in this chapter about ERGs. What is your view on ERGs?*

Caroline: *ERGs are brilliant. Regardless of our differences, it is lovely to connect with those who have the same experiences as you, but be careful, as it does create silos. Allyship is the key – you need to have a culture of allyship.*

You must also have executive sponsorship at leadership level to hold leaders to account and have the conversation. Executive sponsorship is the only way to really help leaders better understand the topic and

> *the ERG group purpose. If there is an ERG group in a corner with no voice or executive sponsorship, what is the point if they are not being represented in the boardroom? Equally the board cannot choose one ERG voice over another.*

Vikki: *Do you have any final thoughts to summarise?*

Caroline: *This is the decade of disruption and it is here. We are waiting to see who will be the brave new sustainable brands. This will be the point of change. We need to bring together multiple human experiences and build on intersectionality.*

> *I do not believe anyone is an I&D expert – how can you be? The world has changed so much you do not know everything about everything – no one does. One source of intelligence is to bring older and younger people together to learn from each other!*

> *The range of different diversity groups is exhaustive. With people experiencing different things based on their background, as people move around the world so freely living in different nations and cultures, the diversity of teams working together becomes greater. But it is inclusion, how people feel included in the group in which they work.*

Vikki: *Thank you very much, Caroline.*

I discussed nationality and working in different countries with Nichelle Appleby, an employee who is classed as an expatriate, someone who lives outside their native country. Nichelle discussed her experience and offered some tips for the ex-patriot community.

Vikki: *Nichelle, when I met you, I was so curious about your own experience of being an ex-patriot. Thank you for sharing these experiences with me – it will help many others to better understand this diversity group. We discussed your experience of being a Black American expatriate living in Germany for work. What has been your experience?*

Nichelle: *Living in Germany is a wonderful and strange privilege. It is also my literal dream come true. I spent the first part of my career working with a traditional American company hearing of leaders being sent to far-off places to shape the future of a team or build whole departments.*

When they returned home they had more than earned their praise, while enjoying an overseas experience. Their return guaranteed them further opportunities, almost all being promoted right away. I hoped one day the opportunity to be an expat in Europe would come after hard work and recognition and it did not seem to be such a lofty goal. I had travelled that far for my graduate degree, obtaining an MBA from Webster University in London, which at the time had a relationship with Regent's College (now Regent's University). Plus, famous Black American artists have moved overseas, and to Europe in particular, for more than 100 years. In the early 20th century and post-World War II, many artists, such as Lois Mailou Jones (France), Audre Lorde (Germany) and Tina Turner (Switzerland), made their way to Europe, contributing their talents and living their own version of the 'European Dream' for short periods of time or indefinitely.

My own ambition and feelings that my work should speak for itself kept me blind to how nearly impossible it would be to reach my goal working within an American corporate system. According to CNN Business, Black professionals in 2018 held just 3.3 per cent of all executive or senior leadership roles, which are defined as within two reporting levels of the CEO, according to the US Equal Employment Opportunity Commission (Sahadi 2020). Since most expat assignments are given to leadership roles, or those poised to be in leadership, Black professionals have almost no access to this type of work opportunity that could change the trajectory of their careers. If lucky enough to work for a company that still assigns Americans to overseas offices, Black Americans are left to fight for scarce spots usually without the same sponsorship or support as their white peers. And that is if they even know the opportunities exist.

My naivety of this issue kept my excitement strong and goals intact. After returning home with a graduate degree, I looked to restart my career with plans to rise in the ranks and to find an expat assignment. My hopes were quickly dampened as my American corporate experience proved disappointing. As I watched certain peers be praised for their efforts and given access to build relationships with executive leaders for mentoring opportunities, I found myself at times ignored and dismissed, my own Director rarely even saying good morning to me. After being told directly that my pay was 10K less than a team member with three years less experience and no graduate degree, all because the consensus at my hiring was that I would be 'happy' for the large pay bump, I felt like my corporate dreams (and my financial wealth) would be dashed.

I was not completely deterred and, due to a large project that needed every hand it could get, I was eventually sent on a two-week trip to China and Singapore to help launch a global project. Normally a job well done on a project of this scale would lead to another challenging project and even a promotion, and it almost did. But when the opportunity for a new project came before landing back stateside, and was then taken away just as fast, I was hurt but not crushed. I would just keep moving forward.

As my career progressed I continued to do great work and experience the negative impact of a lack of diversity, real biases, and almost no inclusion. I was insulted (literally) and endured many microaggressions such as inappropriate comments about my hair and being characterised as 'too' vocal. I continued to be the only Black person in the room and, although it was not uncommon, it was becoming a little harder to bear. I needed to prove myself double time, all the while my peers, all white, were able to move into better positions with real influence and decision-making power, with the salaries to match. Before I knew it I was ten years into a career and stuck. Although years before the CNN report, I was experiencing first-hand how and why Black professionals were not making it to the top.

Ever the optimist, I decided to take a different path, turning to 'out of the box' ways of reaching my goal. After presenting an idea for me to work from an overseas office, including discussing all of the benefits and risks for the organisation, I was turned down. It was time to get drastic and I started looking for remote work. Soon I was a 'digital nomad', travelling Europe for two years while working from my laptop. Finding out later that a peer at my former company was allowed to make a move with her husband and keep her job stung a little, but it was ok. My two-year journey landed me in Germany, married, and jobless. My personal life was just about perfect but what could be next for my career?

In a country where I still have a hard time pronouncing simple words after an entry-level German course, stretching into my full potential at a German-based company would be an accomplishment, but I was starting from a positive base so my hope kicked in. My American and marital privilege allowed me to get a working visa in less than an hour. My education would be honoured without question and I had many years' experience. But there were still signs continuing my career in Germany would not be easy. Would companies take me seriously if I could not conduct an interview in their language? Also, would I experience the same I&D issues here? When I looked to see if my ambition of being a true business leader in this country was possible, there was only one example, Janina Kugel, the former CHRO of Siemens. Every company I wanted to apply to had executives that were all male, all white, and all German. I could not even find statistics on minorities in leadership roles in Germany. If I thought it was harder at home, I was about to be proven wrong. Moving to Germany would make my ascent into my professional potential an even greater challenge.

Much to my surprise and excitement I was able to find an English-speaking role. It is not a deep development opportunity, there is almost no upward trajectory, and my pay is 20 per cent lower than in my previous US role, but I am working in my profession in a new country and this matters.

And that is what is like being a Black American expat. Privileged enough to find work in your new city in your native language, but still plagued by the issues of long histories of lack of true inclusion and diversity in the workplace. As Europe sees new enterprises formed daily and talent becomes more precious in certain fields, creating an environment where leaders with influence and power understand how to see differences as the very strengths that bring about industry-altering innovation is imperative.

Vikki: *Employee Resource Groups are created to support different diversity groups. What is your experience and view on them?*

Nichelle: *These (ERG) groups can be a wonderful way to ensure employees of different and specific backgrounds can find each other and feel a sense of belonging in subgroups. When the people around and above you do not share your experiences of life and work, and never take the time to understand your unique view, you are left isolated. You are human and you need connection. If lucky, employees can find it in these groups. One successful example of pioneering ERG groups is at Xerox, which had the first recognised corporate ERG in the United States (Bathea 2020).*

Although ERG groups can be great, they are not enough. These groups must also create channels for people of different backgrounds to showcase their skills and gain access to decision makers. Executives must be on the lookout for great talent, everywhere, checking their own biases and preconceived notions of certain groups, and give different people a chance to shine. There must be real strategy and action to ensure these groups and networks are integrated into how they develop great talent from everywhere. Organisations also need to develop leaders who are aware and conscious about how they operate in a diverse environment and how to build inclusive workplaces. Even with Xerox leading the way, it was 40 years before Ursula Burns became the first Black female CEO of the S&P 500 company (Umoh and Garrett 2020). If this is any indication of how long it takes to break the barriers for minorities, young European companies must get started.

In the essay 'The master's tools will never dismantle the master's house' Black, female, queer, American writing powerhouse Audre Lorde comments on the lack of women of colour from various walks of life speaking at a conference she was invited to attend. Her frustration in the essay is felt with the way white feminists did not see the need for women of colour, poor women and lesbian women to speak on various topics, not just their specific experiences, to help reform feminism. It is from this essay I take the below quote:

Only within that interdependency of different strengths, acknowledged and equal, can the power to seek new ways of being in the world generate, as well as the courage and sustenance to act where there are no charters.

(Lorde 2020)

Vikki: *Thank you for sharing your story as an expat and a woman of colour. There are so many expats out there, navigating their career in strange countries, where there is an assumption that they 'just fit in'. What would you finally say to our readers?*

Nichelle: *If I may be so bold, there is a great need to create a new world and ERG groups can unleash this creation. Inclusivity is about recognising that we should not relegate minority groups to discussing topics of importance in small groups away from the people who affect real change. These normally ignored experiences and differences can and often do create something new. In other words, it is not just a question of whether employees with disabilities have a chance to connect with others that may share their experience, or if they can help make a more accessible product, but how they can make a brand more viable in ever-changing and saturated markets.*

    Since institutions, organisations and businesses are a core part of how the world operates, leaders must seek out opportunities to help innovate the world we want to live in. Leaders will only be successful when they learn how to truly include everyone and harness their strengths as power to go where no one has gone before, leaving behind what no longer suits everyone to build a better world.

Vikki: *Thank you for sharing your experience.*

Neurodiversity is another diversity group that makes up a combination of different thinking. People who are neurodivergent may differ in mental or neurological function from what is considered typical or normal, frequently referenced to autism, dyspraxia, dyslexia – that is, not neurotypical.

In a *Financial Times* (2019) special report, 'Health at Work', Naomi Rovnik discussed how 'Hiring more "neurodiverse" workers can pay dividends. Companies discover that autistic people and the different way their brains work can be a valuable addition to their workforce.'

I met with Nathaniel (Nat) Hawley, from an organisation called Exceptional Individuals.

Nat: *Neurodiversity brings rich value to the organisation. It brings diversity of thinking and opens up conversations, to bring a different approach in.*

There is no right or wrong way of thinking. The common way of thinking tends to be the dominant way. As a neurodivergent person, we have to learn to adapt to that way, however our views and voices need to be heard to hyper-shift innovation. It is no surprise that 40 per cent of self-made millionaires are dyslexic because they have to find new methods of learning.

Organisations need to look at their own processes and if they do not include this group, they are not being inclusive. You are potentially ignoring a different perspective – for example, we know that one plus one equals two. But it could also be seen as one plus one is eleven. This might be seen as wrong, it is just wrong in the typical sense, but question what you refer to as wrong. This different way of think-ing can bring you innovation and with 7 per cent of the population (potentially your customer) being neurodivergent, your workforce should reflect the people you serve.

With the different elements these values can bring, we need to embrace it, rather than always want to streamline, slim things down and create an 'A to B' process. Take computers: they have a code and if you go outside the code it does not work, but if you can break the rules, you will create amazing experiences. The future needs to embrace neurodiversity and if you get somebody who is neurodivergent, by bringing this together you are building your own quantum computer.

As a neurodivergent person, it is very important to have a space where you can talk and communicate to others, so you do not feel alone or the odd one out; instead, you feel part of the team. I felt very alone and iso-lated until I met others; when I met others like me it gave me confidence.

It is difficult to bring change – how do you innovate when the sys-tem is working for the dominant group which is working for them? A dream team allows you to work to your strengths and prosper because of your neurodiversity, not despite it.

Personally I love being neurodivergent, though it is a pain when you are starting out in your career, but when you harness the benefits of your own unique mindset, it becomes your USP.

Vikki: *Thank you, Nat.*

In a *Financial Times* (2020b) article, John Thornhill states: 'Attitudes are changing as employers come to see neurodiverse people as a human asset that society should treasure, not as a liability to be marginalised. Neurodiversity, which is both a neurological concept and a social movement, is emerging as the "final frontier" in the diversity debate.'

Summary

There are many diversity groups and I have mentioned only a few here, but it is important to note that people do not fit into one group. Learning about each other and respecting that we all come from different diversity groups will energise the workforce and create a learning environment about diversity, and ultimately create inclusivity. But we must look at our behaviour first and ask ourselves, 'Are we being respectful and inclusive of each other?'

Further resources

Interviews

Nichelle Appleby.

Caroline Casey, Founder of The Valuable 500.

Nathaniel Hawley, Head of Community, Exceptional Individuals – Neurodiverse Recruitment and Job Support.

Vusa Tebe, I&D consultant.

Publications

Bathea, A. (2020). 'What Black Employee Resource Groups need right now'. https://hbr.org/2020/06/what-black-employee-resource-groups-need-right-now. 29 June.

Financial Times (2019). 'Health at work', Special Report, Naomi Rovnik, 21 November.

Financial Times (2020a). 'Diversity leaders', Special Report, Janina Conboye, 18 November.

Financial Times (2020b). 'Neurodiversity can empower the workplace', Opinion, Social Affairs, John Thornhill, 26 November.

Lorde, A. (2020). 'The master's tools will never dismantle the master's house'. *The Selected Works of Audre Lorde*. Ed. Roxane Gay. New York, NY: W.W. Norton & Company, pp. 39–45. Print.

Sahadi, J. (2020). 'After years of talking about diversity, the number of black leaders at US companies is still dismal'. 2 June. https://edition.cnn.com/2020/06/02/success/diversity-and-black-leadership-in-corporate-america/index.html.

Umoh, R. and Garrett, B. (2020). 'Black in business: celebrating the legacy of black entrepreneurship'. 3 February. https://www.forbes.com/sites/ruthumoh/2020/02/03/celebrating-black-history-month-2020/?sh=4f4b82542b45

PART 3
BEHAVING AND LEADING INCLUSIVELY AS A LEADER

CHAPTER 8
HOW TO FOCUS ON INCLUSIVE BEHAVIOUR

In this chapter we will look at how behaviour underpins inclusion. Behaviour determines how inclusive we are, which in turn determines how we embrace diversity (B.I.D. = Behaviour, Inclusion, Diversity). We will discuss how inclusive behaviour can positively shift inclusion and diversity.

I prefer to discuss the 'B' (behaviour) before the 'I' (Inclusion), before the 'D' (Diversity)... B.I.D., as I hold the belief that if we

Behaviour – Inclusion – Diversity

begin with our own behaviour and recognise how inclusive we are, we can then decide how we embrace diversity.

What is behaving inclusively?

'Behaving inclusively' is how an individual behaves towards others by listening with curiosity, learning about their backgrounds and experiences, especially how they are included in workplace conversations.

Why is it important to behave inclusively?

Organisations recognise the need to become more inclusive in their approach, in order to bring collective intelligence together where people feel more included, respected and empowered to share their ideas. Sharing ideas more can lead to better innovation and creativity, enabling greater diversity of ideas and the fostering of an environment conducive to innovative thinking.

It is important to champion inclusive behaviour as it builds a better working environment in an organisation, bringing more collaborative styles, such as empathy and listening to others. Setting this approach enables individuals to challenge ideas as they are made to feel more included and able to contribute to the discussion. Acknowledging other ideas can also make individuals feel good and can inspire them to want to generate more ideas.

Is behaving inclusively good for business?

Behaving inclusively has become more prevalent in organisations. There is an increasing amount of research focusing on the topic and strong evidence supporting the business case for inclusive leadership. For example, Bourke and Dillon's (2018) review offers a strong indication of the benefits of leading inclusively, linking it to business growth and higher performance. These benefits include the experiences of others when being led by those who adopt an inclusive behaviour, such as individual feelings of inclusion increasing by 70 per cent, specifically: fairness, respect, value and belonging, psychological safety and inspiration. This in turn enables the company to increase team performance by 17 per cent; increase decision-making quality by 20 per cent; and increase team collaboration by 29 per cent.

How do we become conscious and aware of behaving inclusively?

Traditionally, decision making in the workplace began with senior individuals commanding those beneath them who complied with their instructions, often described as a command and control style. Dating back to the early 1900s researchers began to investigate a different approach, moving the characteristics of traditional approaches and framing it as a more 'inclusive approach'.

By becoming conscious and aware of others, regardless of experiences and backgrounds, this consciousness and awareness will enable individuals to feel included, which will bring more innovation to their work. This can create a sense of greater autonomy and a deeper involvement.

There can be potential obstacles when organisations are not conscious of behaving inclusively, and these obstacles need to be addressed in order to create a more inclusive environment. For example, look out for those who:

- become caught up in their own way of thinking
- are unable to see anything beyond their own thinking

- are too busy talking to let people share their ideas
- may feel threatened or irritated by people because they may think they are better than them
- close other ideas down so that theirs are the only ones heard and likely to be considered.

Integrating inclusive behaviours into leadership development practices

Learning the tools to behave inclusively should be integrated into all leadership development practices. By omitting inclusive behaviour training from current leadership development practices, organisations are not fully producing great leaders for the future. Not making the training relevant to today's workplace could stifle business growth by missing out on the innovation and creativity that inclusive behaviour fosters. There is a range of theories and models available that incorporate an 'inclusive behaviour' as part of broader leadership development.

All leadership development programmes, usually generated by the talent and leadership development teams within HR, should include training on how to behave inclusively in the organisation's current practices. In addition to existing leadership development practices that include inclusive behaviour training, there are also tools that are dedicated to inclusive behaviour training, such as Dillon and Bourke's (2016) 'Six Signature Traits of Inclusive Leadership'. This recognises the importance of solely looking at inclusive behaviour.

If you are not raising the awareness of inclusive behaviours, you will not create an inclusive environment

Dillon and Bourke's (2016) tool proposes that behaving inclusively is vital to the way leadership is executed, demonstrating that six signature traits can characterise an inclusive leader. By exploring the six signature traits, we can link it to behaving inclusively:

- **Curiosity:** Because different ideas and experiences enable growth
  - This goes to the heart of diversity of thought: by bringing together different ideas, people will learn from each other and discover growth in themselves and the organisation's offering.

- **Cultural intelligence:** Because not everyone sees the world through the same cultural frame
  - People from different cultures will see things differently. If there is a problem to be solved, the more diversity there is within the team, the more likely it is that you will find more ways to solve the problem, because of the way people see difference based on their own cultural frame.
- **Collaboration:** Because a diverse thinking team is greater than the sum of its parts
  - By bringing different perspectives together, you create something that is bigger than the sum of its parts. It is this difference in thinking that can go above and beyond the topic in hand.
- **Commitment:** Because staying the course is hard
  - Diversity is hard. Stay on course, remind yourself of your purpose, and put smaller steps in to achieve the milestones so that you can see your progress. This will help you stay the course.
- **Courage:** Because talking about imperfections involves personal risk-taking
  - When others show their imperfections, and show vulnerability, it shows that they are human. They are prepared to share something which enables others to get to know them better. This can create a sense of trust.
- **Cognisance:** Because bias is a leader's Achilles' heel
  - Leaders who are not aware of their own biases are missing out and can potentially make the wrong decisions, which can lead to mistakes.

It is important to be aware of traits that might hold inclusive leaders back, such as:

- looking for acceptance
- surrounding themselves with familiarity
- accommodating others too much
- internalising problems
- having a higher need for harmony and a lower need for achievement and status
- being likeable to others and holding in frustrations rather than upsetting relationships.

Such traits may also make it difficult when leaders come under pressure to operate in a fast-paced, quick decision-making environment, which may not be conducive to behaving inclusively. For example, inclusive decision makers may be slowing processes and decisions down, while the more command-and-control leaders may be quicker in their decision making.

Taking other people's views into consideration in regard to decision making may take longer than one person making an autonomous decision. The pace of decision making may not align with the organisation's pace; however, making the wrong decision if it is quick and not thought through may have an adverse effect on the organisation. It is important to recognise the pace of the organisation. It can also be argued that operating in such a fast-paced environment can be the 'death of inclusion'.

While it is with good intent that an inclusive decision maker wants to include everyone's views, there needs to be a clear understanding in matching this slower pace with the organisation's needs. The organisation must be clear that if they want to adopt a more inclusive leadership style, certain processes may need to slow down to achieve more effective results. This will enable a more thorough, inclusive and methodical approach to their processes, rather than a quick turnaround and short-term decision making that may not result in the best outcome. For example, if a critical role needs to be filled quickly, the organisation needs to weigh up how long that role can stay empty for versus hiring quickly, in which case it is likely that the organisation will reach out to the same network to replace like with like and not consider more diverse candidates who it may take longer to find. Diversity is hard. It takes time, but when an organisation allows itself to take the time, it will reap the benefits by building a more diverse organisation.

Unconscious thinking when working in a fast-paced organisation

The times we need to act quickly, think fast, up against time pressure, and need to move on to the next thing can be problematic. When we fast-track our thinking, our brains move quickly to the solutions we know, without properly spending time on assessing the options, so we may not get to the best decision. This can have a negative impact on business growth, client solutions and how employees are treated. Taking time over the decision may entail including other opinions and views, and this may take longer, but it might get us to a better solution.

By nature, we are not always open-minded: our brain quickly assesses who to trust and who we need to be cautious about. A negative assessment may trigger a fight-or-flight response in our behaviour.

Be conscious when you 'fast' think and when you 'slow' thinking down

When we slow our thinking down, we are more conscious, controlled and make a higher effort in our thinking. By slowing down our thinking, we are more likely to remove our biases about others. With fast thinking, unconscious bias can be more present. When we speed up our thinking, the brain makes quick judgements and assessments of people and situations. This can prevent us from making objective decisions.

Biases are shortcuts to make it easier for us, and as a result it is even more important to be aware of the decisions that are made and what the consequences might be of them. Decision makers need to constantly challenge themselves in their thinking and be conscious of what, if any, biases may occur as a result of these shortcuts.

Mindset

In order to focus on behaving inclusively, we first need to look at our own mindset: what is set in our mind and how conscious or unconscious we are of it. Our mindset determines our actions, beliefs and behaviour. Leaders must learn about their own mindset before understanding what is needed to embrace change, otherwise it will be ineffective.

What is a mindset?

The term 'mindset' refers to the patterns of our mind, or frames of reference. A mindset reflects 'personally distinguishable attitudes, beliefs and values, which influence one's ability to learn and lead, and to achieve and contribute' (Buchanan and Kern 2017). First, we need to explore and become aware of our own mindset, then look at ways to adapt it. If the mindset is not adapted, it can become resistant to change. As organisations need to encourage inclusive behaviour, there could be concern about those leaders who may not be willing to adapt their mindset, especially if those leaders are likely to be in a position of authority and making daily critical decisions.

Fixed and growth mindsets

Dr Carol Dweck (2006) has undertaken extensive research into mindset, focusing her work on the 'fixed' and 'growth' mindsets, defined as follows: the fixed mindset creates an urgency to prove yourself over and over, whereas the growth mindset is based on the belief that your basic qualities are things you can cultivate through your efforts.

Satya Nadella, CEO of Microsoft, applied this concept of growth mindset to solve a real business problem. When Nadella took over Microsoft, he recognised that a lack of growth and innovation was due to its dysfunctional behaviour as an organisation. Microsoft explored these behaviours, undertaking research firstly to diagnose what was inhibiting growth and innovation. Having gained a better understanding of the issue, they were then able to move to a solution which shifted the environment into being more inclusive in their behaviour.

Nadella's awareness of this concept and adoption of it demonstrate that he was prepared to commit and take action to enable more inclusive behaviours within Microsoft, resulting in a more inclusive and much healthier environment. Such a shift reaps huge rewards, as it has an impact on attracting and retaining great talent and ultimately benefits customers by facilitating more innovative solutions. All of this results in a more profitable, open and collaborative culture.

Having a better understanding of the fixed and growth mindsets can help leaders to determine which one they identify with and how their behaviour impacts others as they lead organisations. As discussed earlier, mindset is a powerful lever for change and many organisations are in constant change. According to Dweck (2006), the key differences between the fixed and the growth mindset are the following: a fixed mindset leads to a desire to look smart and therefore a tendency to avoid challenges, give up easily, ignore useful feedback and feel threatened by the success of others. As a result, a person with a fixed mindset may plateau early and achieve less than their full potential. Comparing this to a growth mindset, Dweck explains that this leads to a desire to learn and therefore the tendency to embrace a challenge, persist with any setbacks, learn from criticism and find inspiration in the success of others. The two are very different and can determine the success (or not) of an individual.

According to these definitions, leaders that possess a growth mindset may be receptive to learning and to adapting their behaviour. They may be conscious of people's differences. Based on this thinking and their willingness to learn, they may be curious about what skills other people can bring and therefore be more inclusive. Leaders that possess a fixed mindset may not be open to being inclusive of other opinions and may exclude others.

This approach can be successful, as Nadella proved at Microsoft, but only if an organisation is committed to investing in such a concept, potentially moving from a traditional leadership style (command and control) – fixed – to becoming more inclusive (inclusive leadership) – growth. First, decision makers need to increase their own awareness of inclusive behaviour and understand what it means, before they can identify how they may need to change their own behaviour in order to manage their teams inclusively.

Table 8.1 is an example questionnaire you can use to determine whether leaders have a fixed or growth mindset.

Table 8.1 An example of a 'fixed or growth mindset' questionnaire

Circle the number to indicate how far you agree or disagree				
	Strongly Agree	Agree	Disagree	Strongly Disagree
1. Your intelligence is something very basic about you that you can't change very much	0	1	2	3
2. No matter how much intelligence you have, you can always change it quite a bit	3	2	1	0
3. You can always substantially change how intelligent you are	3	2	1	0
4. You are a certain kind of person, and there is not much that can be done to really change that	0	1	2	3
5. You can always change the basic things about the kind of person you are	3	2	1	0
6. Music talent can be learned by anyone	3	2	1	0
7. Only a few people will be truly good at sport, you have to be born with it	0	1	2	3

Circle the number to indicate how far you agree or disagree				
	Strongly Agree	**Agree**	**Disagree**	**Strongly Disagree**
8. Maths is much easier to learn if you are male or maybe come from a culture that values maths	0	1	2	3
9. The harder you work at something, the better you will be at it	3	2	1	0
10. No matter what kind of person you are, you can always change substantially	3	2	1	0
11. Trying new things is stressful for me and I try to avoid it	0	1	2	3
12. Some people are good and kind, and some are not; it's not often that people change	0	1	2	3
13. I appreciate when people give me feedback about my performance	3	2	1	0
14. I often get angry when I get feedback about my performance	0	1	2	3
15. All human beings without a brain injury or birth defect are capable of the same amount of learning	3	2	1	0
16. You can learn new things, but you can't really change how intelligent you are	0	1	2	3
17. You can do things differently, but the important parts of who you are can't really be changed	0	1	2	3
18. Human beings are basically good, but sometimes make terrible decisions	3	2	1	0
19. An important reason why I do my work is that I like to learn new things	3	2	1	0
20. Truly intelligent people do not need to try hard	0	1	2	3

TOTAL:

How did you score?

Strong growth mindset	=	45–60 points
Growth mindset with some fixed ideas	=	34–44 points
Fixed mindset with some growth ideas	=	21–33 points
Strong fixed mindset	=	0–20 points

To develop more of a growth mindset, consider the following:

- Acknowledge and embrace imperfections – hiding from your weaknesses means you'll never overcome them.

- View challenges as opportunities to grow and learn.

- Try different learning tactics and strategies – there is no one-size-fits-all model for learning, so figure out what works best for you.

- Be aware that the brain is not fixed, which means the mind is not fixed either.

- Replace the word 'failing' with the word 'learning'. Consider looking at the word 'FAIL' as First Attempt In Learning.

- Stop seeking approval – when you prioritise approval over learning, you sacrifice your own potential for growth.

- Cultivate a sense of purpose – Dweck's research shows that people with a growth mindset have a greater sense of purpose. Keep the big picture in mind.

- Disassociate 'room for improvement' from 'failure'.

- Take and provide regular opportunities for reflection.

- People with that extra bit of determination will be more likely to seek approval from themselves than from others.

- Use the word 'yet'. Dweck says 'not yet' has become one of her favourite phrases – that is, I have not done that 'yet'.

- Ask for feedback – challenge yourself by asking others to evaluate your performance on a regular basis. Respond to their comments constructively and use them to help you improve.

- Take ownership of your attitude – once you develop a growth mindset, own it. Acknowledge that you are someone who possesses a growth mentality and be proud to let it guide you.

How can we educate leaders in inclusive behaviour?

There needs to be some form of intervention or training in place for individuals to become aware of their own behaviours and mindsets, otherwise change may not take place. Creating and conducting an intervention is important in helping individuals to increase their awareness of their own behaviour before focusing on inclusion, otherwise they may not be aware of when they include or exclude others.

How does your behaviour impact others?

Self-awareness is critical in leadership since leaders must understand how their behaviour impacts others. Starting with this simple question can get leaders to begin to think differently: 'How does your behaviour impact others?'

Asking this initial question can help leaders to better understand how they are behaving towards others and make them more aware of their audience (the receiver). Figure 8.1 indicates how individuals should attempt to understand themselves and the impact they have on others.

With the diversity of people in the workplace, it makes business sense for leaders to become open to learning more about different cultures, so that they can embrace difference. If they do not embrace difference they will ignore a proportion of their workforce. This model can play an important role in raising leaders' self-awareness.

If we do not raise our self-awareness, we will not be aware of our blind spots. Korn Ferry (Zes and Landis 2013) undertook a research study to identify the 'blind spots' in individuals' characteristics (a blind spot is a tendency not to see other perspectives), and the frequency of such blind spots was then gauged

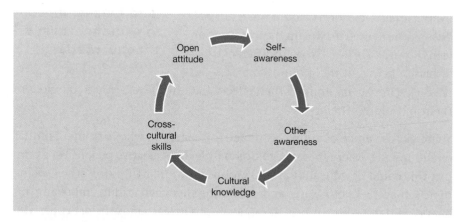

Figure 8.1 The journey to cultural agility

Source: Adapted from Janakiraman, 2011.

against the rate of return (ROR) of those companies' stocks. The analysis demonstrated that, on average:

- Poorly performing companies' employees had 20 percent more blind spots than those working at financially strong companies.

- Poor-performing companies' employees were 79 percent more likely to have low overall self-awareness than those at firms with robust ROR.

(Zes and Landis 2013)

This research is indicative of the benefits of raising self-awareness and demonstrates its importance for those who are in decision-making roles. Leaders must understand that today their decisions have wide and far-reaching ramifications for people they will never know.

What happens when we are not conscious of our behaviour

Being unconscious of our behaviour can be detrimental to ourselves and potentially others. We may have biases towards people and situations, and we may make assumptions of others without backing these up with evidence. This is dangerous.

First, we need to recognise the biases we have. Everyone has some form of 'bias'; this is normal. 'Bias' is a term used to explain the way a person leans towards a belief. There are different types of biases; being aware of our own biases can

Remove assumptions and biases; move to evidence-based conversations

have a big impact on limiting their effects, but only if we become conscious of them and address them.

Some biases can be as simple as preferring someone who is from a familiar environment because there are commonalities between two people. For example, this could be educational background or similar thinking styles. Being more self-aware of our biases and addressing them can lead to embracing difference and respecting others. It can enable us to learn more from people who are different from us and learn about their differences.

By becoming more conscious of our own thinking, we can better understand how and why we behave the way we do.

Inclusion nudge

'Recommend the leaders to take some of the Implicit Association Test to spot their biases. Inform them that seeing own behavioural patterns (incl. biases) helps the brain change behaviour'

Our unconscious thinking happens automatically and is where our biases can occur without us realising. Our brain is triggered to make quick judgements and assessments of people and situations. These are influenced by our own background, cultural environment and personal experiences; these, in turn, drive our behaviour in particular ways. A danger of being unconscious of our biases is that we may gravitate to 'the familiar', such as choosing our friends based on a common background, cultural environment and personal experience. This is an example of where we have an affinity bias towards a specific type. In a workplace setting, this can be dangerous because it fuels 'homogeneity' as we remain comfortable with what we know. It encourages similar thinking, leading to the exclusion of those who are not in that group.

Examples of unconscious thinking

Think about when you drive a car – are you really conscious of what you are doing or are you so used to it that your unconscious thinking kicks in as you change gear and check the wing mirror? When you arrive at your routine destination thinking, have you really been conscious of your driving? Your thoughts may have been on the day ahead or the previous day, so you were consciously thinking about something else while your unconscious thinking drove you to your destination! This is how powerful unconscious thoughts can be.

An unconscious thought may arise from the past and just slip out as you speak, and sometimes this could potentially offend someone. You may think: 'Where did that come from?' This represents a form of historical data that you gained from your own experiences, but also from the experiences of family, friends and society in general. While we may not think we are prejudiced, whether that is racist, sexist, ageist, ableist, or anti-religious, our families might have held these prejudices and some of the language associated with these opinions can become embedded in our unconscious mind. You may find yourself blurting out or repeating something you heard your parents or grandparents say, without necessarily understanding the point or comment yourself; but if you fully understand the comment you might choose not to express it consciously. Similarly, children repeat words or phrases that they've picked up without being sure of what they mean: this is unconsciousness behaviour.

Below are two stories of well-known CEOs who became wealthy due to their success, but, because of not being considerate or even conscious of their actions, they fell.

The Ratner story

In the UK, there was the famous slip that Gerald Ratner made. As stated in the media at the time of the event: in 1984, at the age of 34, he took over the British family firm Ratners. The firm had 100 shops, most of them loss making. The shares were worth 27p, but within a couple of years they rocketed to £4.20. He streamlined and accumulated, discounted and marketed the products. By the time he was 40 years old, Ratners was the biggest jeweller in the world with 2,500 shops. On one occasion he was due to make a speech, addressing 5,000 members of the Institute of Directors at the Royal Albert Hall, London. He spoke with a lack of conscious thinking: 'We do cut-glass sherry decanters complete with six glasses on a silver-plated tray your butler can serve you drinks on, all for £4.95. People say how can you sell this for such a low price? I say because it is total crap. We even sell a pair of gold earrings for under £1, which is cheaper than a prawn sandwich from Marks & Spencer. But I have to say that the sandwich will probably last longer than the earrings.' He was not conscious of what he was saying and certainly not conscious of the consequences. He later filed for bankruptcy.

The McDonald's story

Chief Executive Steve Easterbrook stepped down after he had a consensual relationship with an employee against company rules. As stated in the media at the time of the event: the policy was in place, and Mr Easterbrook did not abide by it. He later acknowledged the relationship and said it was a mistake. 'Given the values of the company, I agree with the board that it is time for me to move on,' he explained.

Easterbrook had helped grow the fast-food company and was widely credited with revitalising the firm's menus and restaurants, remodelling stores and using better ingredients. The value of its shares more than doubled during his tenure in the US.

These stories indicate that regardless of how successful a CEO is, they can be brought down quickly. When someone is derailed from top leadership it is not because of a lack of business literacy or skills, it is because of lapses in judgement and questions about their character. I would say these two stories show lapses in judgement.

The conscious mind rationalises thoughts that occur in the unconscious mind. The first step in addressing unconscious biases is to discover which ones you have. Bringing them to consciousness allows you to begin the process of undoing unconscious thinking habits. Removing or simply being aware of any unconscious biases helps to heighten the quality of your decisions.

> **If you are conscious of a bias you have and you do not let it go, then be careful that you are not holding on to a prejudice**

If there is a fight between the unconscious and conscious mind, the unconscious tends to win. Our brain puts information into categories, and this information becomes suppressed and almost buried. The conscious brain processes 45 bits of information per second. The unconscious brain processes 10 million bits per second. There lies the power.

How to recognise when people around you are playing out their biases

Being aware of when people around you are being biased will help you better understand situations.

Different types of bias

Below are examples of different types of bias.

Status quo bias: keep it safe

This is when people just keep it safe, keep things the same, which can have a negative impact on the pace of change in business or decision making. It can also contribute to homogeneity when everyone just nods in agreement. If we all just agree with each other there will be a lack of diversity of thought among a group leading to a lack of creativity and innovation. 'If it is not broken, why fix it?' may have a negative impact on any business decision.

Negative bias: watch out for negativity

Be mindful of the amount of bad news coming your way: for example, in the media there is more coverage of 'shocking, negative or crisis' news, which makes it seem more 'worthy'. We give it more credibility, without truly understanding the evidence.

Projection bias: I project my belief onto you

This is where people assume that you are thinking the same as them. They may even ignore information they are given and select information that only fits with their beliefs. Respect the uniqueness of each individual and the views they bring, rather than projecting your views onto them.

Current moment bias: discounting information in the past or the future

This is where people only concentrate on the information they have right now in front of them. The more data and evidence you have, the better your decision making will be.

Affinity bias: I like you because you are like me

Affinity bias is when there is a natural tendency to gravitate to someone who is like us. This may be in our appearance, thinking style or educational background. We may seek approval from these people because we like them and feel comfortable in their presence. The more aware we are of this, the more we can consciously reduce our bias towards similarity and look for difference.

Exercise: The echo chamber

Who are the five people you go to when you have a problem that needs solving? If they are similar to you and to each other, you are likely to get similar resolutions to your problem. The best thing to do is to reach out to five very different people who are also different to you in order to find a diverse set of solutions to your problem.

Did you know. . .

- Less than 15 per cent of American men are over 6ft tall, but almost 60 per cent of corporate CEOs are over 6ft tall.

- In the 30 years since blind auditions were introduced in the US, the number of women in orchestras has increased fivefold (despite insistence by recruiters that they had no preference for male or female musicians).

Association bias: stereotyping and prejudging

Association bias is when there is an association of people with certain stereotypes. This may be women with art and design, older people with being slower and resistant to change, men with technology. The more aware we are of this, the more we can consciously reduce our bias and think differently, and not make assumptions.

Selection bias: unconsciously selective about specifics

Selection bias is when there is specific data a person is drawn to noticing, ignoring other data that is not important to them at that moment in time. Attention bias can also be known as 'selection bias'. It is like buying a red car – afterwards, you see many other red cars. It is because you become conscious and aware of them. Red cars have always been around but you notice them because the colour has become more relevant to you. It is easy to think this is because the information is now occurring more frequently, but this is not the case. You have a bias to select it. This selective behaviour is now getting your attention.

When you decide something is true, you look for facts and evidence to confirm it is true.

I believe this is true about me, so I will find facts that back it up

We can become so fixed in our beliefs, regardless of what the data says, that even if contrary evidence is in front of us we will make it fit our belief. The risk is that we will not check the veracity of things we believe in, as we see our belief as the truth.

Unconscious bias in meetings

Meetings tend to run in the same format, with the same people speaking up. An inclusive leader will recognise this and encourage everyone's voice to be heard. This will ensure the meeting is open and objective. An inclusive leader will also be conscious of the make-up of their team and decide whether their teams are diverse enough to bring enough different thinking to the meeting. One of the most common mistakes that organisations make is to run meetings with individuals from the same mould. It may bring short-term success, but it will not give the strength and depth to enable the organisation to survive and adapt to changing circumstances. I have seen organisations fail because this has been their blind spot.

De-biasing organisational processes

Processes are everywhere in an organisation. Processes can also hold bias, because they are made by humans. The best thing an organisation can do is to 'de-bias their processes'. Look at each process and find ways to de-bias: if people can work in a system which is free of bias, then practices will be operated in a fairer and more transparent way. Figure 8.2 shows some processes you may wish to look at and make inclusive.

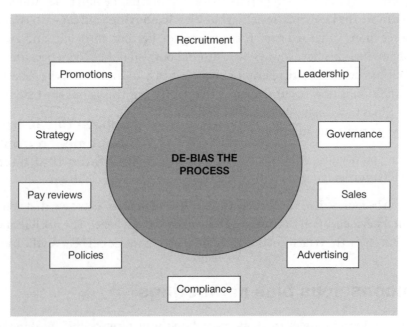

Figure 8.2 Organisational processes to review when de-biasing

Can we combat bias?

We can be conscious of combatting bias through the following techniques:

- Be curious about your own unconscious biases – we all have them.
- Treat your first impressions as a hypothesis, a test.
- Notice when others make assumptions.
- Believe everyone is equal.
- Focus on how individuals are different from their stereotypes.
- Take another perspective.
- Interrupt yourself and challenge your own thinking: Why are you thinking in that way? Can you think in a different way?

It is important to help your colleagues recognise that everyone has biases and to explain this to them in a non-threatening way. This is not about blame as biases are something we are all probably unaware of until we see them for ourselves. We don't know what we don't know.

How can we value difference?

First, we need to know what to do with difference. Different people will bring different things, explanations, language, experience and knowledge.

Because we may not be used to dealing with difference, we may react to it by feeling a lack of understanding or feeling uncomfortable, and we may find we have a limited vocabulary to talk about the subject at hand. This is in large part why it can be difficult to understand the world around us when it is becoming so diverse.

People in the workplace may find themselves in situations that they have not had experience in, so it is important to understand what the reaction will be when confronted with new experiences. Leaders are more and more likely to shy away from these experiences rather than confront them, for fear of saying

If I am a man, how do I respond to the #metoo campaign? If I am white, how do I respond to the Black Lives Matter movement?

the wrong thing or being asked a question they may not know how to answer. When working with leaders, it is important to start with the conversation of how confident they are in reacting to different and sometimes new situations.

Experiential learning

One of the best ways to combat biases is to step into somebody else's shoes, so experiential learning is incredibly valuable. For example, if you work with a col-

What experiential learning can you do in the workplace to enrich people's understanding?

league who is a wheelchair user, until you sit in the wheelchair, navigate around the office, bathrooms, lifts, door entrances, you cannot begin to understand your colleague's experiences.

How confident are we when responding to difference?

The following exercise helps individuals test how confident they are when responding in the moment to certain statements.

Exercise: Responding to difference

How confident are you in your reactions to difference? Think about your immediate response to the statements below, and give each one a score of 1 to 4 according to the following answers.

Answers:

1   I would avoid responding.

2   I would be uneasy in my response.

3   I would be fairly confident with my response.

4   I am completely confident, no problem.

Statements:

1   Your white male colleague tells you that his son is now at a disadvantage in the workplace because of all this diversity stuff that is going on.

2   Your colleague, a woman of colour, gets the promotion you wanted and felt you deserved. She comes up and tells you how excited she is.

3   Your assistant tells you she feels suicidal.

▶

4 A female team member asks you if she can take a day off because of her period.

5 A male colleague tells you he needs time off for mental health reasons.

6 An interview candidate arrives at the office and they are a wheelchair user.

7 A colleague is undergoing gender reassignment and asks to be called Diana.

8 Your colleague tells you: 'I have just interviewed two applicants with the same skills, knowledge and experience. I am going to appoint the one that comes from an underrepresented group to help our diversity.'

9 You are told that women are hired for accomplishments while men are hired for their potential.

10 I have to reach my target for gender diversity, so I will employ the woman over the man.

Add up your scores from the 10 statements:

0–15: You are at the beginning of your journey. Ask yourself why these situations make you uncomfortable.

16–30: Continue on this journey. Think about what has got you to this point. Why are you comfortable responding to some of the statements and not others? Is it because of your personal experience?

31+: You are making great progress on your journey. There could be an opportunity to share with others how you got to this place. Use the fact that you feel comfortable to start conversations around diversity.

Dominant and non-dominant groups

Those who are in non-dominant groups may have better negotiation skills because of how they constantly navigate through the dominant groups. An example of someone who is from a non-dominant group would be the only woman on a board where the rest of the members are men. Individuals operating within non-dominant groups may think more flexibly, adapting their language, style and approach. Individuals who mainly operate in dominant groups may not need to focus so much on being flexible. They do not need to as they are among individuals that are like them. Dangerously they all may think alike, leading the group into homogeneity in their style. This can be the opposite of creativity and innovation. Homogeneity is a business risk because of this.

As dominant groups begin to form, they start to become 'exclusive' and may not recognise, or recognise too late, that there is a lack of diversity and ultimately diverse thinking. Gravitating to like-minded people answers a human need: we gravitate to people who are like us and we begin to build a sense of belonging, which is one of the greatest human needs.

When being a dominant person in a dominant group, be very careful of your thinking patterns, as group thinking might occur and a lack of understanding may be present without being conscious of it.

Further Resources

Bourke, J. and Dillon, B. (2018). 'The diversity and inclusion revolution'. *Deloitte Review*, Issue 22, January, pp. 81–95. https://www2.deloitte.com/content/dam/insights/us/articles/4209_Diversity-and-inclusion-revolution/DI_Diversity-and-inclusion-revolution.pdf

Buchanan, A. and Kern, M.L. (2017). 'The benefit mindset: the psychology of contribution and everyday leadership'. *International Journal of Wellbeing*, 7(1), pp. 1–11. doi:10.5502/ijw.v7i1.538

Dillon, B. and Bourke, J. (2016). *The Six Signature Traits of Inclusive Leadership: Thriving in a diverse new world.* https://www2.deloitte.com/content/dam/Deloitte/au/Documents/human-capital/deloitte-au-hc-six-signature-traits-inclusive-leadership-020516.pdf.

Dweck, C. (2006). *Mindset.* New York, NY: Random House. (First published in the UK by Robinson, 2012.)

Janakiraman (2011). *Inclusive Leadership: Critical for a Competitive Advantage.* Princeton, NJ: Berlitz Languages. http://www.tmcorp.com/SiteData/docs/BerlitzWP_InclusiveLeadership04%20(2)/d977154a6d924bd1ee1423da3b51f040/BerlitzWP_InclusiveLeadership04%20(2).pdf

Nielsen, T. and Kepinski, L. (2016). *Inclusion Nudges Guidebook*, p. 37.

Nielsen, T. and Kepinski, L. (n.d.). Implicit Association Test. Project Implicit. https://implicit.harvard.edu/implicit/takeatest.html

Zes, D. and Landis, D. (2013). *A Better Return on Self-Awareness.* The Latest Thinking, 18 November, pp. 10–12. https://www.kornferry.com/content/dam/kornferry/docs/article-migration/Briefings17_TheLatestThinking.pdf

CHAPTER 9
HOW TO BE INCLUSIVE WHEN COMMUNICATING

In this chapter, we will focus on how we can be inclusive when communicating. Language is a powerful tool: we may use thousands of words per day, mostly unconsciously because of the speed with which we operate in the workplace. We will discuss the impact of how we communicate, and how we can still be inclusive with our language even when we're working against time.

What is inclusive language?

Inclusive language is free from words, phrases or tones that reflect prejudiced, stereotyped or discriminatory views of particular people or groups. It does not deliberately exclude people from being seen as part of a group. A commitment to inclusive language is an important attribute of a modern, diverse and inclusive society. Inclusive language enables everyone to feel that they are being reflected in what is being said. Opposite to this is discriminatory language, where a person or a group of people treats others less favourably or says something that has a less favourable effect on others because of their personal characteristics.

Why inclusive communication is important

Language is usually our main form of communication in the workplace and it plays a powerful role both in contributing to and in eliminating discrimination. Language that is exclusive is harmful because it can inhibit or prevent people reaching their full potential and simply offend them. The individual themselves may become so used to being 'labelled' into a certain category that they end up behaving that way. For example, if a child is repeatedly told they are not intelligent, they will begin to believe it and their behaviour will align with their belief.

When individuals are categorised into a group there becomes a tendency to judge them, leading to a standard being pushed onto that group. This can lead to one group being seen as better than the other and therefore segregation begins. This is the death of inclusion because once segregation begins, other groups may not feel the need to learn about each other, impacting teamwork and performance in a workplace setting.

Being appropriate in our communication

To some, there may be confusion about what is, or is not, appropriate language. If unsure, the rule of thumb is not to use it. This could mean avoiding using language that comes across as derogatory, insulting, sexualised or aggressive. It is always worth checking in with a colleague whether your communication is acceptable. This enables us to learn from each other, raising awareness and educating each other.

We need to be curious so we can learn
The difficulty in today's world is that we are unsure what to say at times, and some, mainly leaders, do not say anything on sensitive topics, as they tend to avoid the conversation, which can build a gap between individuals. This can result in exclusion, with our vocabulary being limited as a result of not being curious or brave enough to approach a particular topic.

Communicating inclusively is simply constructed in ways that treat all people with respect. There is no place for prejudiced, stereotypical or insensitive references to people based on their characteristics or background. Organisations should by now be in a position to have simple values that allude to equity, respect and inclusion, and be committed to equal opportunity and access for every employee regardless of their background. Inclusive communication plays an important role in acknowledging and treating everyone equitably, with the sensitivity and respect to which they are entitled.

Discriminatory communication is damaging to others and we need to be aware of the diversity of those we are communicating with: differences may include culture, race, ethnicity, gender, sexual orientation, age, ability, socioeconomic status, physical appearance and where they live. Used with care and sensitivity, language can play a powerful role in minimising conflict and building connections between individuals and groups. In this way, it can play an important part in building a society in which all people are valued and feel included.

Words can also be our most dangerous weapon. We want to aim to build our vocabulary to be more inclusive, so that we can embrace the diversity around us.

Think of someone who you gravitate to because of the language they use. What is the tone, status and make-up of that person?

We often hear the words 'you speak my language' or 'we speak a common language here'.

Remember, being curious about difference can help you to become more inclusive. Aim to increase your sensitivity.

The unwritten rules

Think about the first time you took your friend or partner to meet your parents. What did you warn your partner about? What did you tell them to say or not say?

Organisations have just as many unwritten rules. An individual's success can be determined by how quickly they learn these rules, and whether they learn them at all!

Consider the following: in different cultures it may be the norm when meeting other people to exchange chit chat and banter or to observe formality; to ask questions or not to ask questions. These are subtle inequities that can be harmful and will put individuals at an advantage or disadvantage in the workplace.

Think of someone who apologises frequently and someone who interrupts. What is the background of these two people? There is no right or wrong. It is just part of someone's cultural upbringing.

The silent have something to say

When in a group setting, we should be looking for different ideas, yet some members of our team may be staying silent; there may be individuals who are not speaking up, not because they lack ideas. Think of someone who does not speak up. Do you notice at the time that they're staying silent, or do you not notice?

We cannot assume a quiet individual does not have an opinion. The aim is to ensure all individuals are invited to give their opinion. If we rely on those who raise their voices, we may be marginalising our creativity and ideas within the group setting.

Tips to help you become more aware of your language

- Do not 'objectify' or 'single people out' in a way that they might find awkward.
- Take responsibility for the impact you have on others – you might think you are being straightforward or direct, but the person you are speaking to might hear 'threatening' or 'aggressive' language.
- Avoid using 'minority' as a blanket term for people from underrepresented groups in the workplace. They may be a minority in a working environment (similar to being non-dominant), but outside the workplace, they may not be a minority.
- Jokes related to someone's visible or cognitive diversity are unacceptable; judging a workplace audience is difficult and jokes should be avoided.
- Avoid using jargon that excludes people who may not have specialised knowledge of a particular subject. We can slip into using jargon words or acronyms, especially when operating as a dominant person in a dominant group. This excludes those who do not know their meaning.

Historical language: masculine and feminine language

Historically in the English-speaking world, language usage has privileged men and often rendered women invisible or inferior. It is important to be aware of the historical use of language, and to change to a more equitable way of speaking. Historical examples can be found in:

- the dominance of male-related terms
- the unequal treatment of men and women
- the stereotyping of gender roles.

Avoid patronising expressions. For example, instead of 'the girls in the office' use 'our employees in the office'. Use alternatives for 'man' and 'he/him/his' where the term is generic. For example, instead of:

- 'mankind' try 'people' or 'humanity'
- 'manpower' try 'workforce'
- 'manning the office' or 'manning the stall' try 'staffing the office' or 'staffing the stall'
- 'sportsmanlike' try 'fair' or 'sporting'
- 'The employee may exercise his right to a review' try 'Employees may exercise their right to a review'
- 'Chairman', when referring to the generic role of the person chairing a meeting, use 'Chair'.

Equipping yourself to use inclusive communication

We need to ensure that we are present in the moment so we can be conscious of the language we use. For example:

- Be engaged and make sure you are welcoming.
- Allow for silences. This can be uncomfortable for some, but silence helps you be more effective with the words you choose to use. It gives you time to think and reduces the risk of talking over other people.
- Ask questions to learn more, showing your curiosity.
- Invite people to contribute to the conversation and to your idea, so that you prevent them losing interest in what you're saying.
- Allow three seconds after a person stops talking to ensure they have not just paused and that they have finished.
- Be cautious with humour – it does not always translate across cultures and without the benefit of verbal tone can be misunderstood. When in doubt, leave it out.
- Segregating words such as 'ladies' or 'hi guys' can come across as patronising; instead use 'people' or 'all'.

- Allow people whose first language is not English to speak too and do not rush them.

- Ask the quieter people for their thoughts, and encourage the team to explore those ideas.

If you are leading meetings, take the responsibility of setting up an inclusive environment, where you explain up front that all voices will be heard, and all contributions will be considered. You may want to allude to how powerful language is so that the attendees think about the words they choose to use. This will bring more consciousness to those around you when they think about their own language and what they might wish to contribute.

CHAPTER 10
HOW TO BE AWARE OF OUR OWN BEHAVIOUR WHEN WORKING WITH OTHERS

In this chapter, we will explore how individuals can help or hinder when working in groups and how group dynamics can play out when working with diversity around them. We will learn how to address these dynamics and be more conscious of each other when working in groups.

Groups work in a 'system', which is a set of things, or a structure that people are connected to. When bringing together the system and the individual, these then become interconnected, so it is important to look at not just the individual behaviour within a group, but also the system in which they operate.

Some organisations have had systems, such as processes or ways of working, for years. Through the years, 'stuff' will have been added to the system, potentially making it clunky and building up biases within it. Once we can begin to understand how systems work, we can explore how people's behaviour patterns are integral to the many systems in which they belong. By focusing on the system as well as the individual, we can identify the build-up of biases and then begin to look at how to 'de-bias' it, focusing on 'de-biasing the system' not just 'de-biasing the individual'.

Individuals have multiple group memberships and belong to different systems and groups. When individuals come together as a group, working within a system, it is important to explore what is influencing their behaviours, to identify how inclusive the group is. This can be referred to as group dynamics, which is a collection of people's individual behaviour as a group member and how they impact the whole group. The individuals within the group will have their own purpose as to why they are there and it is important to explore what this is.

Forming a group

When a leader is setting up a group, in order for it to be a success from the outset it is crucial that the leader is conscious and curious about the diversity of the group. If a leader has a higher understanding of inclusion and diversity, they are more likely to set it up for success, enabling safety, diversity of thought and collaboration.

They will be conscious of the make-up of their team and decide whether individuals are diverse enough to bring different thinking to the group. One of the common mistakes organisations make is to form groups with individuals from the same mould. It may bring short-term success, but it will not give the strength and depth needed to enable the organisation to survive and adapt to changing circumstances.

Building an inclusive group with trust

The more inclusive the group, the more likely it is that trust will be present (Figure 10.1). Trust means different things to different people, but trusting each other can enable individuals to comfortably give their views and opinions, which can be beneficial to the organisation, creating a rich and diverse dialogue. It can also mean that where there is trust, there is a likelihood that individuals can show some vulnerability, bringing their authentic selves to the group.

When bringing a diverse set of people together in a group, the organisation needs to build a culture of inclusion. First, they will need to focus on why each individual is part of the group and why they have come together:

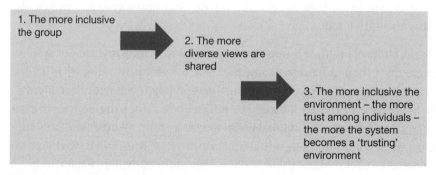

Figure 10.1 Inclusion grows trust

- What are we here to achieve and why?
  - Agree the outcome you want to achieve.
- What is the objective of the group?
  - Agree your purpose.
- What is the objective of the individual?
  - Be clear in your expectations.
- How do you ensure all voices are heard?
  - Behave in an inclusive way.
- How do you ensure all views are included?
  - Listen respectfully.

Setting these group goals will give clarity and alignment, regardless of individuals' backgrounds. Once individuals are clear on what they bring to the group, they can start to build the trust which mobilises them to help each other. When individuals begin to raise their own awareness of each other, they can become conscious of the group dynamics around them. The aim of inclusion is for individuals to bring their diversity of thinking to the group and feel they can share their different views without experiencing exclusion.

Once the safe space is created in the group, rich conversations can be had, allowing everyone's view to be heard and considered. The more diversity of thought in the group, the more likely it is that creativity and innovation will happen. This is why it is important when creating a group that we bring different types of backgrounds together.

Group dynamics

A lot of the dynamics are often played out under the surface. Whenever someone's behaviour changes the group dynamic, it will either help or hinder the group.

- No single behaviour is bigger than that of the group.
- The more conscious we are of this, the more likely the dynamics of the group will be positive, working in an inclusive style.
- If the inclusive style is not present, individuals with more diverse ways of thinking may leave the group.
- The group may then be exposed to group thinking and homogeneous conversations.

- This can lead to a lack of creativity and innovation which organisations require in order to stay competitive in their market as they face accelerating transformational pressure.

Behavioural problems in groups that encourage exclusive working environments are difficult to pin down, but, if not dealt with, they may become part of the group culture which then becomes harder to shift. If the group dynamic becomes negative, this can result in individuals within the group not experiencing inclusion and they may refrain from sharing the unique knowledge they hold. The group will then lack quality and rich conversations that would bring them to better solutions.

The group is only as strong as the weakest link   If there is one behaviour that negatively impacts the group, it needs to be challenged and potentially removed. It just takes one behaviour in a group to change the dynamic, either negatively or positively. Also watch out for individuals navigating their way through to get an outcome that they believe is the best one. A selfish person who is non-inclusive is a weak team member.

Putting in place useful strategies can maximise the potential of the group. Below are a few examples:

- Include a 'way of working' practice.
- Call out challenging or excluding behaviours quickly.
- Enable the group to have a collective voice.
- Discuss what you are all here to do that you cannot do without each other.
- Identify the development journey the group needs, not what they want.
- Create an interest in what everyone has to say.
- Become more curious about the system that the group is working within.
- Raise the group's understanding of the system.

To achieve these points, a process model can be used to set helpful ground rules, such as the CLEAR model (based on Hawkins 2017):

- CONTRACT

  With all individuals in the group – agree outcomes, purpose and expectations of the way of working

- LISTEN

  To each other's views, the group dynamic and the context

- EXPLORE

  Emerging patterns and experiment with the different views shared

- ACTION

  Choose a way forward – create an action plan that shows diversity of thought

- REVIEW

  Actions and get feedback from other diverse groups

As individuals operate in a group, they need to bring their diversity of thought to the conversation, feeling safe enough to do so. Bringing in difference helps innovation and creativity, yet achieving inclusion goes beyond just bringing a set of diverse individuals together in a group. Inclusive groups that are diverse in their thinking can really excel, leading to better business decisions and the implication of this can be a higher-performing organisation.

Table 10.1 demonstrates what to look out for with a diverse and/or an inclusive group. It demonstrates why you need both. Inclusion. . . *and* diversity. The environment must be one of trust and safety so the implications are that any individual can come into the group and recognise this trust and safety, bringing their diverse opinions with them.

By building trust and a safe environment, we can then explore whether there is a need to restructure the system we work within and, if so, look for leverage points for change. The implication of not creating this trust and safety is that individuals will soon recognise that as they come into the group they will need

Table 10.1 A model showing the disadvantages and advantages of having both inclusive and diverse groups

	Cohesive teams	Diverse teams
Advantages	● High trust ● Ease of decision making ● Ease of communications ● Collective accountability	● Top talent ● Good skills spread ● Idea generation ● Challenge to status quo
Disadvantages	● Risk averse ● Weak innovation ● Weak personal accountability	● Misunderstandings ● Coordination and communication ● Building trust

Source: Owen (2017)

to conform to the groups way of thinking and adhere to the system. This does not create behaviour change for the good.

Creating a safe environment

To create a safe environment, focus on safety and trust so individuals feel secure.

- Create safe spaces to hold conversations.
- Allow individuals' voices to be heard.
- Ensure all views are considered.
- Become conscious of the implications that your behaviour has on others.

By creating safe environments, the organisation can gain more effective results by bringing the group together with one purpose. Groups will be achievers if they have a common purpose; a group of individuals do not have to get on well because the purpose will draw people together. Trust is the invisible glue that keeps groups together. Only when it is missing do we discover how important it is and how hard it is to create it.

Trust enables a group to bridge challenges and can be the biggest determinant of success or failure. It can drive individuals' performance if they feel they can trust the group members, based on their credibility, shared values and experiences.

Invest time in building trust between individuals The implication of building a safe environment is that it can lead to a high-performing culture within the group. Boundaries can be pushed when individuals are given encouragement to speak up and be included within a group; if everyone has their say it can lead to better decisions and higher commitment. There are no shortcuts to building the sort of trust where everyone feels confident enough to express themselves.

A group can create value beyond the individual by staying dedicated to the purpose. Individuals can hugely help the learnings of a group; the more contributions to the group, the more diversity of thought and different opinions will be shared, enabling others in the group to learn from each other. This creates the value.

How to open up when working with others

It is good to understand how authentic (or inauthentic) you come across in a group and how you show up in your behaviour. People like to see the human side of each other, especially when working together – it can help to build trust.

However, it is important to be aware of how your behaviour can impact others. Understanding how you come across and what you might hold back is a good start. Then ask yourself after each point below, 'why is this?':

- If I expose the 'real me' I might lose control.
- No one asks for my advice.
- I have to be better than others.
- If I delegate, I will lose control.
- This is the way I am; I cannot change.

You can also do more than just look at your own behaviour: encourage other people to recognise how their behaviour impacts others, helping them to work together in a non-threatening way.

Individual behaviours can have an impact on the performance of the group and ultimately the organisation and its culture. A group that is functioning well together can help individuals with their learning and development. If this

What are we here to do today that we cannot do without each other?

learning is hindered, this will have a detrimental impact on bringing about change. Groups need investment as they are made up of individuals, ideally diverse, bringing their unique and different opinions to the group. Therefore, it is critical to invest from the start and provide clarity as to why the group has come together – the purpose. It is the individual behaviours that create the dynamics within the group and these in turn will determine how successfully the wider environment performs.

Individuals are often assembled into a group, becoming cross-functional and bringing collective intelligence together. The potential to draw learning from the group must be greater than the speed of change. The more inclusive the environment, the more likely it is that individuals will be open and bring their views to the group, giving them a competitive advantage by staying ahead of the curve. By getting ahead, the group will be able to innovate and shape the future, challenging the status quo. This can be done effectively in an inclusive and trusting environment.

Individual purpose versus the collective purpose

The more aligned the individual's purpose is to the group's purpose, the more likely it is that they will come on the journey with you. If the purpose is created behind closed doors and presented to the group, it is less likely that individuals will buy into it.

Belonging to more than one group and being agile in your behaviour when moving between them

The more open to diverse thinking we are, the more able we are to move between groups. Individuals belong to a number of different groups, and the more agile we are in our thinking, the more mobilised we are to move around. If we show up in only one way and listen to our preferred way, we are not putting ourselves into a learning space and we are limiting our ability to move between groups. We need to show that we can think agilely enough to embrace the views of others. By embracing the views of others, we can then become more inclusive in our approach, when working in these groups.

Do you stop and give enough time to notice others' reactions?

By becoming more agile in our thinking, we can become more curious. For example, you may be in a meeting and think to yourself: 'Why is it that only men are asking the questions? It is making me curious.'

Becoming agile and more curious in our thinking enables us to learn more about ourselves. The more self-aware we are, the more we notice other individual's reactions.

Notice the following:

● What is the group sharing, and how agile are you in your thinking about this?

- This can be the data shared, how responsive you are to this data and how you might embrace the data to help you think differently.
- What experience are you having?
  - Be conscious of your own feelings: what are you feeling, what are you experiencing in the moment? Are you feeling comfortable, motivated, included or are you experiencing discomfort, lack of motivation and exclusion?
- How can you influence to help the group stick to the purpose?
  - Bring the group back to the purpose if you feel they are going off on a tangent. If they are going off course, reset and bring everyone back by reminding them of the reason why you are all here.
- How open are you, and what is your level of ability to work with others?
  - Be conscious of how you are working with others. Are you working better with some people than with others? Why is this – what is making you gravitate to some individuals in the group? Check the background of those you are gravitating to, and those you are gravitating away from.
- How do you come across to others?
  - Ask for feedback and be conscious of your language, body language and the reactions of others when you speak.

Communicating in groups

Raising your own awareness of the different ways in which the group members communicate can help you better support the group by increasing everyone's understanding of these different ways of communicating.

It is impossible to be part of a group and not communicate at all. It is the different communications that shift the group dynamics. Silence is a form of communication, as is body language, and being aware of how the group communicates will raise the understanding of the group. It is important to bring the different communications styles to each other's attention, taking the time to discuss the pros and cons of how these impact the dynamics of the group.

Getting to know each other's communication styles can help the group dynamic – by gaining each other's trust and listening to each other, you can build a more inclusive environment.

It may be the case that communications need to slow down so that everyone in the group can be on the same journey driving towards the same purpose – you do not want to lose anyone on the journey through miscommunication.

Be aware and conscious of negative group dynamics through communication, such as an individual speaking up with a thought that is different to the majority group thought and being ignored, or individuals blaming or scapegoating those who are absent.

Transparency can also drive inclusion in a group setting – the more open and transparent an individual is, the more positive impact it will have. The more secrets there are within the group, the more negative impact it will have.

Fundamentally within a group, individuals will aim to:

- interact with others
- influence others
- share with others
- get a reaction.

A pattern of interaction develops in a group and underpinning this is communication. The more inclusive the interactions are, the more likely it is that the group dynamic will be impactful and effective.

Meeting with the group

There is likely to be a group leader. If they have inclusion and diversity at the heart of everything they do, it will set a precedent of how meetings will run. Below is an example of (1) preparing for inclusive meetings, (2) setting expectations of how meetings can be run with the group and (3) being present.

Preparing for inclusive meetings

There are different ways to prepare for a meeting; be as inclusive as possible so everyone is well equipped ahead of the meeting, and include anyone who may not be able to attend. They will also need the preparation, and the outcomes of the meeting too. Below is an example of inclusive preparation:

- Check with all attendees if they can make the time and date of your meeting.
  - If not, ensure they are briefed so they experience inclusion.

- Share an agenda before the meeting.
  - Encourage participation and allow for attendees to prepare, ask questions and share their thoughts.
- Suggest to individuals that they email anything else that comes to mind after the meeting closes.
  - This may be a preferred approach for some individuals.

Setting expectations of how an inclusive meeting will run

- Rotate who runs the group agenda when they meet.
  - This encourages different leadership styles.
- Remind each other of the group's purpose and why they have been brought together.
  - Map back to 'What are we here to do today?'
- Be supportive of each other by being curious with an open mind and a willingness to grow.
  - Be as inclusive as you can – respectful curiosity goes a long way to enabling an interest in each other.
- Learn from each other, foster team spirit and ask how each other's day has gone so far.
  - This is crucial – you do not know what each other's day looks like before they arrive. Are they fully checked in and present or is their mind somewhere else, because of what happened earlier in the day?
- Do not make any assumptions or hold any biases.
  - Encourage a call-it-out culture where people can respectfully question each other's points.
- Be mindful of each other's cultural backgrounds.
  - This is important when recognising difference in views and also geographical differences.
- Clarify and agree individuals' roles and responsibilities.
  - There is no point having an individual show up to a meeting and not contribute. They need to have the opportunity to add value.
- Be conscious of the gender balance in meetings and ensure there is equal representation whenever possible.

- It is essential to have a balance. It needs to be more than a 'token' one.
- Spend a few minutes at the beginning of the meeting checking in with everyone and clarify that everyone's view needs to be heard.
  - Invite quieter individuals into the conversation.
- Allow for silence. Silence is good, yet it can feel uncomfortable for some.
  - Silence enables others to take time to think. Balance this by keeping the momentum going and taking pauses.
  - Use the pauses to your advantage – these give other attendees time to reflect on what you have said.
- Reaffirm messages to provide clarity.
  - What I have heard is. . .
  - Can you clarify your second point please. . .
- Respect the person who is speaking.
  - If there is a point to put across when someone is speaking, use the three-second rule: allow five seconds after a person stops talking to ensure they have not just paused, but have finished.
- Address interruption in the moment.
  - If someone is spoken over, it is the responsibility of others to politely ask the person to wait until the other has finished speaking.
- Be open to feedback.
  - It is important to be aware of and listen to other points of view.
- Think about the technology features you plan to use: if you put your camera on in meetings, does that mean everyone else has to put theirs on?
  - 'I have put my camera on, but it does not mean everyone else has to.'
  - 'I have to switch off my camera because of bandwidth. Please feel free to switch yours off if you want to.'

And overall. . . be present

- Avoid distractions while on the call; avoid thinking about other things and focus on the moment.
- Be conscious of your body language and the tone of your voice. How are these characteristics coming across and what is the reaction of others?

Inclusion nudge

'Posted on the wall of the meeting room: Is everyone at the table?'

The relationship with yourself and others when working in a group

The group will have a variety of features, such as loyalties, resources and entanglements. Individuals may behave differently in the different groups they belong to. Our behaviour tends to change in different environments. Your stimuli and responses within the group will be dependent on the environment in which you are interacting.

Loyalty

Understanding how you behave in your different groups and how you communicate will determine who you are loyal to.

When an individual leaves a group, it will be their energy they leave behind, rather than their current presence. This is called their legacy. It can be argued that change cannot take place if there is still loyalty to those individuals who have left the group.

Working with others who hold different values

When individuals begin to clash with each other, it can be because of a mismatch of their values. When it comes to cultural differences, these misunderstandings can provoke confusion. This is when we may not be receptive to something that is not familiar to us because it may not align with our own experiences. We may have expectations that are not met, and so we label others as rude or offensive and potentially damage relationships based on our own values.

Being conscious of our own values may help us get to resolution. If you start to notice specific behaviours in yourself or others after a misunderstanding, such as rudeness, disrespect or weakness/lack of confidence, they need to be discussed and resolved.

We are all made up of many invisible traits, and by being aware of our own values and behaviours we will be able to become more culturally competent. By recognising how we react or respond to others based on misunderstandings and working on these reactions, we will become more self-aware and will be more likely to do something about it. You may want to set out expectations among the group, as suggested below.

We expect everyone to:

- demonstrate and celebrate behaving inclusively
- be accountable for ensuring everyone feels included
- be responsible for making our colleagues feel valued
- take personal responsibility for their own behaviours and the impact they have on others
- ensure everyone is free from inappropriate physical contact, derogatory comments or aggressive language.

We do not expect anyone to:

- create a culture of fear
- create a small 'power group' within the larger group where they cannot be challenged
- protect individuals that makes difficult conversations harder.

Calling it out

It is easy to be in situations with others and gravitate to people like us. It can be hard to 'call it out' when individuals are not used to doing it. It is good to agree that by respectfully calling each other out, you are creating a learning environment within the group. This can be seen as 'feedback'. The following are examples of non-inclusive behaviour. If they occur, they need to be called out.

- Blaming or complaining about others
  - Confront the individual and discuss the issue, rather than blaming their actions on someone else.
- Making derogatory remarks
  - People usually have good intent, but be careful if it makes you feel good by putting someone else down. This is not healthy.

- Saying 'They do X because they are from Y'
  - You may be making an assumption based on your own experiences.

Develop your own knowledge

When working in groups, it is important to learn and develop your own knowledge and understanding of inclusion, as it will help you:

- Build a vocabulary for describing others that are different to you
  - For example, heterosexual people may not have the vocabulary to discuss the LGBT+ community, simply because they may never have had the conversation or know someone from that community.
- Build an understanding of how others reach their decisions, how they got there and where they started from
  - Build curiosity and interest in others within the group.
- Identify similarities as a starting point and learn about each other's values
  - Test each other's values and understand why and where they come from.
- Identify differences along the way and be ready to discuss openly to learn more about them
  - Turn the differences into respectful discussions, acknowledging each other's differences and talking about them.
- Understand why selected individuals are involved
  - Why are you here, what makes you want to be part of this group?

Feedback within groups

The meaning of feedback is understood differently across cultures. It is important that you do not just give feedback in the way that you know how. Discuss and decide how feedback will be given in the group. This underpins individuals' learning of the impact their behaviour has on others.

Feedback needs to be:

- evidence based
- specific
- respectful
- timely.

It is important to include training on giving feedback, as it cannot be assumed that individuals know how to do it. This is not the case. It is also important for individuals not just to seek feedback from those they know, who may be like them and have a relationship with them. A more effective way of seeking feedback is to go out to those who are different to you and who see you differently to your network and peers, as well as within the group you work in.

Tips when giving feedback

- Use words that are safe to highlight unintended language or experiences.
- Be curious about the individual when giving feedback.
- Do not create a fear culture when giving feedback – aim to keep your mind and the recipient's mind as open as possible; this is where the learning occurs.
- Do not probe an individual on a topic that they do not have an answer to. This can be intimidating.
- Be objective – back up with examples and evidence.
- Be respectful and confidential when giving feedback. For example:
  - When you did X, it created a reaction of Y.
  - When you said X, it created a reaction of Y.
  - The impact you had on the group was X.
- Educating at this stage can be really helpful, to avoid confusion and misunderstandings. For example:
  - Instead, you may consider doing X.
  - Instead, you may consider saying Y.

These tips will bring an improved outcome and help the group move forward in what they are looking to achieve and their purpose.

Inclusion nudge

'Use automated, real-time communications tools, which are similar to social media approaches, employees can receive instant feedback from multiple sources on their performance. For example: Great presentation in the meeting today'

Further resources

Hawkins (2017). *Leadership Team Coaching.* Kogan Page, p. 85.

Nielsen, T. and Kepinski, L. (2016). *Inclusion Nudges Guidebook*, p. 143.

Owen, J. (2017). *Global Teams*, p. 177. Pearson.

CHAPTER 11
HOW TO RESPECT
CULTURAL DIFFERENCES

In this chapter, we will discuss the importance of respect when working with different cultures. We will also look at how organisations grow globally, but may not invest enough in the cultural elements when people work together (and are thrown together).

Cultural differences and how they come together

Organisations' biggest challenge can be their biggest opportunity – working across different cultures. It can lead to great team collaboration and inclusion, but also huge misunderstanding within the workplace. Sometimes cultural differences can underpin breakups and failures when organisations acquire or merge. Yet, give it the focus it deserves and it can be a huge opportunity in terms of business growth and diversification into new markets.

Paying attention to cross-cultural working and the differences individuals bring can enhance an organisation's performance, resulting in a competitive advantage because knowledge and diversity of thought are brought together. If welcomed, these can bring more innovative solutions to clients and customers.

Respecting cultural differences is a great way for leaders to find differentiators and innovative thinking, which will help grow their products and solutions. The creativity of different cultures can become so rich and exciting, the power can be immense, and the working environment will thrive if individuals are empowered to bring their thinking to the table. It ties people together in groups and allows for rich learning by respecting that we are all different. It is simply critical for the success of any organisation when operating across cultures. Everyone is unique in their ideas and this uniqueness can provide organisations access to rich data.

Developing cultural awareness is a process for everyone; it requires a long-term approach to learn about others. Start by discovering how culturally aware you are. You can do this by raising your awareness of your behaviour around others. For example:

- Notice when you shy away from asking questions about others' cultural backgrounds.
  - You may not have the vocabulary.
- Start by sharing some information about yourself so you can build rapport with the other person. For example:
  - My nationality is. . .
  - I grew up in. . .
  - My hobbies outside of work are. . .

By becoming more aware of different cultures and being more curious about our differences, we can then begin to leverage the opportunities that sit behind it. Those organisations who embrace it will have a better culture of inclusion and diversity. Cultural awareness must be at the heart of any inclusion and diversity strategy.

There is no culture that is better than another, and entering conversations on an equal status helps everyone experience inclusion. Below are some examples of how to become more aware of cultural differences:

- Be conscious of who is speaking up in meetings and who is not speaking.
  - What is the cultural difference between those who are speaking up and those are not?
- Take time to connect with people who are different from you.
  - The lower down the organisation, the more diversity you may find.
- Acknowledge cultural challenges and opportunities.
  - Seek advice from those who are different to you, to help you learn.
- Show vulnerability; discuss your experiences (or lack of) with others about your own cultural upbringing.
  - This brings the conversation out and empowers others to do the same.
- Track over time whose ideas are acknowledged.
  - Is the cultural background of the individuals behind these ideas similar and are there any patterns?

- Ensure there is a mix of cultural backgrounds in presentations, meetings, panel discussions etc.
  - It is important for the rest of the organisation to see cultural diversity too.
- Seek feedback and ideas from those who are different to you.
  - This enables you to gather a diverse range of feedback and identify whether you are different around different cultures.
- Do not be afraid to admit that you have limited knowledge of each other's culture.
  - Break the ice and learn!

You also may want to start to identify how your own network looks. Are they of a similar background to you, or are you conscious about building your network with people of different backgrounds? Look at your LinkedIn profile: how diverse is it?

Inclusion nudge

'Ask: Would my response to that situation have been the same if she had been a he. . . OR. . . if they had 25 years' experience rather than been 25 years?'

Becoming culturally aware

Becoming culturally aware is when individuals gain the ability to relate and communicate across different cultures, understanding the unique differences of others. It is when individuals become curious about others no matter how different they are, giving them the time and space to share their point of view.

When organisations cultivate this cultural awareness, they can build the ability to tap into cultural knowledge and competency. This will enable them to:

- achieve a better return on investment
- enter merging and diverse markets
- be inclusive of *all* talent
- become more innovative and creative, positioning them as a thought leader
- reduce mistakes based on a lack of awareness and understanding of clients and talent.

There have been stories that have hit the headlines over the years of organisations that had a real lack of cultural awareness, costing some of them millions of dollars. This may have been a result of, for example, a lack of knowledge of the local language, unsuitable product design for the market, greeting clients in inappropriate ways, using logos that were offensive in some countries. This would have been down to lack of cultural knowledge and understanding of the market they were looking to enter.

Organisations can no longer create decision-making teams that have a lack of diversity and cultural awareness. Those who are decision makers must be culturally aware enough to lead the organisation into the future.

As we continue to operate in a world where borders are almost invisible, it has brought the business world together. Yet more investment and understanding need to be put into the impact of how individuals operate together in groups as we aim for the same purpose in the interest of the organisation we serve.

Many factors will have brought individuals together: whether it is employees working in other countries, global teams coming together virtually, access to technology platforms, it has enabled us to reach out further.

Taking the time to explore cultural awareness can be advantageous to the organisation and interesting to the individuals. They can learn how to:

- bridge commercial gaps
- increase trust and performance
- diagnose cultural differences and identify strategies to deal with them
- reduce misunderstandings and miscommunication
- resolve differences
- develop new skills and have a broader view of the world.

Yet, cultural competency requires further research and investment. Many cultural traits are hidden: to learn more about each other, it is important to tune into our emotions and recognise how we have been shaped by our own experiences, and to learn about how and why others have been shaped by their experiences.

Taking the focus off yourself and putting it onto the person you are interacting with brings an inclusive style to your approach

By being curious and asking open questions you will be able to listen to an answer that goes beyond just a 'yes' or 'no'. The more agile and open your mind is, the more you will learn about the perspective of others, which will bring richly diverse views. Once you open your mind to learning about differences, the benefits will begin to show. You will find yourself:

- broadening your vocabulary
- expanding your network and 'go-to people', therefore becoming more inclusive
- building an inclusive culture around you
- coming across as inclusive and a good listener
- no longer thinking only in your way but also embracing another way
- respecting others by being more aware of your own cultural belonging and upbringing
- recognising cultural challenges that may arise in others
- de-biasing conversations.

Conscious inclusion

Taking the time to listen and include others is a skill. Turning the attention from yourself onto others, learning how they are feeling and what they are experiencing in the moment can be beneficial to all. It is what you do with your behaviour that is the critical part. Those leaders who step up and show their curiosity demonstrate that they want to raise their awareness of cultural diversity. They will become the role models of the organisation.

Further resources

Nielsen, T. and Kepinski, L. (2016). *Inclusion Nudges Guidebook*, p. 183.

CHAPTER 12
HOW TO RESPOND TO I&D IN TIMES OF CHANGE

In these times of mergers, buy-outs, downsizing, campaigns and pandemics that have shaken our world, we can no longer ignore these movements and changes. If such change is left to chance, and organisations are not focusing enough on culture and inclusion, they will lag behind as a business.

A 'forced change' is good for the evolution of our society. There may be good reasons for organisations to merge, buy, sell or downsize, but if there is not enough focus put on the culture and inclusion, the deal will fail. Over the years we have read examples of how companies fail because of cultural misunderstandings and diversity issues.

A prime focus during any change must be put on how newly formed teams work together, who gets the top jobs, how customers will be treated and how different cultures will play out. If an organisation just focuses on the 'cost and cash' as its priority, it will be in it for the short term.

If an organisation focuses on the cultural aspect as much as on 'cost and cash', it can transform and have an opportunity to evolve with real diversity of thought creating innovation and creativity. For example, if an organisation has bought a company in an emerging market, then it makes sense to have the representation of this market at the leadership table. It is surprising how few companies really understand this and go through a transformation only to come out the other side with a lack of diversity in their representation. Building diverse leadership teams across the organisation during transformational times creates more innovation and creativity for its clients.

As an organisation goes through such a transformation, it needs to be conscious of the make-up and background of those employees it retains and those who leave the business. It becomes a business risk if great people with different thinking leave or are not included in decision-making discussions.

By taking the opportunity to drive diversity of thinking, an organisation can:

- reflect its client base
- retain the best talent and discover new talent; every new (or changed role) is a chance for talent to shine
- have diversity of thinking during and after the transformation
- build a more diverse talent pool to have a future-ready diverse organisation.

If this is not achieved, an organisation may take a backward step and:

- encourage group thinking and have a lack of diversity of thought in critical decision-making meetings
- not provide an attractive place to work as a result of homogeneity
- lack the ability to problem solve
- lack innovation and creativity
- provide an 'exclusive' place to work, rather than an 'inclusive' place to work
- reduce diversity of teams, impacting their ability to perform and reflect their clients, with the risk of losing them
- risk losing business through a lack of understanding of how business is conducted in the new market due to lack of cultural understanding.

It is important for an organisation to ensure that it stays at the forefront of diverse thinking. Employees will be very aware of the changes and will be curious about what the change will mean to them. Will they still have a job? What will this mean in terms of any promotion or future prospects? The organisation must act on the uncertainty that employees may experience as a result of change. Below are steps to consider during times of change.

Take time to watch and listen as a leader

- Take time to watch and listen carefully to your employees, as change (or even anxiety over impending change) can unsettle your employees and negatively impact the workplace.
- Sometimes employees may express their anxiety directly to you, but at other times their anxiety may become apparent through changes in their

behaviour or performance. This is especially the case when change threatens their comfortable and stable routines.

- Take time to observe and listen to the pulse of your organisation, and then take steps to deal with the anxiety that you may detect.

Demonstrate your genuine concern

- Great leaders realise they cannot achieve their goals if their people are not performing at their best. Employees, especially in times of stress and challenge, look to leaders for solutions.

- As a first step, be an example of transparency and honesty. Open the lines of communication between you and employees. Talk openly and regularly about what you know.

- Show you care about your people's welfare by understanding their concerns.

Fix what you can

- Often, uncertainty results from miscommunication or misunderstandings. Fix the things that you have control over.

- Take the initiative to fix whatever you can as quickly as you can.

- If you find the problems caused by change are beyond your scope, avoid promising your employees things you cannot deliver.

- Talk to your high potentials and invest in those who are flight risks.

- Consider offering alternative employment methods. For example, 'ramping off' encourages employees to consider a reduced working schedule, which can help diversify teams that have been established and together for a long time. By offering an alternative approach to working life, you can unleash opportunities for other diverse thinking to come into the decision-making processes.

Be positive and look for opportunity

- Remain positive. Challenge your employees to show initiative and seek out solutions, new ideas or cost savings.

- By encouraging them to take the initiative you help them to keep moving forward, focusing on what can or might be done.
- Inspire people by presenting a compelling vision for the future.
- Inspire and empower your most powerful ambassadors.

What to look out for as a leader through the transformation

- What will be the new group dynamic?
- Given the talent mix on the current team after the transformation, what will be new or unique?
- What will the team look like in terms of people from different backgrounds?

Where organisational power lies

By growing organically, organisations may become huge power structures, and it is this structure (the system) that employees are expected to work within. Power can be found with a specific group in various parts of the organisation. By being astute to where the power sits, you can save time and energy when confronted with it. Where this power sits will have a huge impact on an organisation's ability to include and/or exclude.

Power generally sits at the top of an organisation and a 'dominant group' is formed. This may lead to 'power games' being played out and behaviours becoming territorial due to the group members wanting to obtain more power both as a group and as individuals. The dangers of too much power lying in one part of an organisation are that:

- individuals within the power group may not wish to share, but rather withhold information and compete for power
- individuals may not want to relinquish power outside of this dominant group to others in the organisation because they feel their control is under threat
- inequality appears and those who are not part of the dominant group or do not have a share of the power are less likely to have access to opportunities that become available.

In an ideal world, power would be shared out more broadly and deeply, creating a stronger feeling of trust and a collaborative approach. One effective approach is for an organisation to review and analyse where the power sits and identify ways to transfer it to other individuals who also have the ability to take their slice of power and *em*power others, allowing power to be more evenly distributed. A power transfer model could be put in place to allow organisations to avoid getting to a point of 'greed' (Table 12.1).

If an organisation is bold enough to be this inclusive, it will see a transformation in its profit and performance. Once it has identified potential leaders who think differently and have different backgrounds, by starting to transfer elements of power and decision-making responsibilities to them, the organisation will be able to rebalance and mobilise a range of different areas within its business.

Implementing the power transfer model takes collective agreement and understanding. It is not about an individual; it is about mobilising the system to become more innovative and creative for clients and customers. How quickly or slowly decisions are made will depend on those who hold the power.

Table 12.1 A power transfer model

Too much power	Distributing and transferring power
● Protective attitudes ● Lack of knowledge sharing ● Competitive behaviour	● Open ● Share knowledge ● Share information ● Collaborative behaviour
Creates: ineffective business growth	**Creates: effective business growth**
● Guarded behaviour ● Slow decision making ● Lack of trust	● Different skillsets that aspire to change ● Transform the business to face accelerating transformation pressure ● Transfer power to different teams and individuals to achieve a more innovative approach
● **Creates: excluding behaviours**	**Creates: high-performing teams**
● Do not include those that may be a threat ● Make biases and assumptions about others	● Transparent ● Inclusive and inviting ● Curious about others ● Backgrounds, styles and behaviours come together to inspire employees and clients

The power is where decisions are made

The key to the approach is to identify those leaders who hold the power, yet do not lead or behave inclusively. 'Who holds the power' will need to be addressed.

Forced change

'Forced change' is needed. It can be created by movements that spin out of crises. Take COVID-19 – I&D practitioners will tell you that the effort to encourage organisations to consider remote working has been a long journey. Some organisations do not embrace remote working; some label it as 'flexible working for mums', or 'you can work from home on a Friday'. But it goes much deeper than that. For employees to have flexibility in their working day is so valuable, for many different reasons.

The reasons will vary depending on people's needs and backgrounds, but here are a few examples:

- Primary and secondary care givers:
    - I need to pick the children up from school.
    - I need to take them to an appointment.
    - I need to check in on my parents.
    - My pet needs to be let out/go to the vet.
- Religion:
    - I need to pray but the offices are not suitable and inclusive for my needs.
    - I am fasting.
    - I am celebrating my religious day.
- Medical appointments:
    - periods
    - menopause
    - IVF
    - health scares
    - regular check-ups (dentist, doctor).

This flexibility is sometimes referred to as 'work/life integration', a situation where employees are able to keep their lives running while doing their day job. It is a core reason why many employees continue to work for their organisation when it empowers them to integrate work and life. One way to describe this is to say that the organisation uses an 'adult/adult' approach, rather than a 'parent/child' approach.

I spoke to Sara Hill, Founder and CEO of Role Mapper Technologies, a platform to design and manage inclusive jobs that unlock talent and diversity.

Sara: *86 per cent of leaders believe offering remote working improves talent attraction and/or retention (Management Today 2020). Before the pandemic, there was a workforce trend towards increased flexibility. It was, and is, the #1 benefit when seeking a new employer. Eighty per cent of workers would turn down a job that didn't offer flexible working. One thing we can confidently state is that the pandemic is radically changing how organisations view work, and it is also changing how employees view and engage with their work. Some organisations have started their journey by creating flexible workplaces, but others still have quite a way to go. This isn't just a 'women only' requirement either. More and more men are looking for more flexibility, with around 60 per cent of working fathers saying they would prefer to work part-time, if it meant they could still do meaningful work and rise in their careers. According to Timewise (2020), 60 per cent of employees want to continue remote working post-lockdown, which means that, as 'normal' working resumes, employees will continue to demand more flexibility around how they engage with work.*

The business benefits of flexible working:

- up to 125 per cent increase in female candidates
- 80 per cent increase in quality hires
- reduces employee turnover by 80 per cent
- 30 per cent uplift in applications when job ads state they are open to flexibility
- increased productivity.

Further resources

Interview

Sara Hill, Founder and CEO, Role Mapper Technologies.

Publications

Management Today (2020). 'Is remote working sexist?', Orianna Rosa Royle, 20 October.

Timewise (2020). 'Up your remote working game with psychometrics'. Thomas International.

PART 4
BUILDING AN I&D APPROACH WITH LEADERS, EMPLOYEES, CUSTOMERS AND SUPPLIERS

CHAPTER 13
HOW TO ENGAGE LEADERS

Engaging leaders is critical. It is very typical that leaders will sit up and begin to engage when you talk about the business case, data points and the risk, and also 'what's in it for them'.

When I work with leaders, the biggest conversation is: 'How do I create business growth and bring this I&D topic into every day?' If you're not linking I&D to your business strategy, do not bother doing it, as it will be seen as an add-on.

But. . . the first thing is to ask leaders: 'Do you really buy into this?' This will help you assess their level of motivation. The more I&D gets on the leadership agenda the better. This needs to be **'Do you really buy into this?'** a regular topic of discussion but the reality is that leaders do not always know how to have the conversation, so they will need to be supported and guided.

Much about inclusion and diversity is engaging with and supporting non-dominant groups, sometimes known as 'minority groups'. In fact, it could be argued that most of the time there is really one 'dominant' group at the top of organisations: men. But they are not engaged enough in the debate; they have a spotlight on them, but sometimes they are unsure how to get involved in the I&D conversation. Yet they have a huge responsibility, and there is an expectation that they will take part and lead the topic because they sit at the top, leading the organisation, which also means leading people. When the leaders originally entered the workplace it may have been a very different environment: nowadays employees are more and more diverse with different expectations.

Once I&D is on the leadership team's agenda (the board, extended leadership team, management team), simply start with the conversation. Below is an example of how to set up a session with a group of leaders to have the conversation around I&D.

Set up a safe environment to have the conversation

Create a safe environment for the group. Ensure the group understands that it is important to sign up to a set of 'rules' which is the agreed way of working in the session set up for them. For example:

- Keep things confidential, to allow openness and honesty.
- Listen to each other with respect.
- Challenge constructively.
- Be open with each other.
- Turn phones and notifications off.
- Let each other finish.
- Give everyone the opportunity to contribute.

By stating this and ensuring everyone agrees, you are setting a common understanding among the group.

Icebreakers are always a good place to start. It is a bit of fun and it enables individuals to hear their own voice before getting started. Below is an example of an icebreaker:

How to create a virtual fruit bowl

- Go round the group and ask each person the same question: 'What fruit would you be and why?'
- As you go around each person, make a note of each answer. It is likely you will hear different types of fruit, such as 'A banana: I do not want to slip up', 'A lime: I can be quite sour at times.' This brings some fun and enables everyone to settle in.
- Once you have asked each person, you can refer to the exercise as a metaphor: 'Metaphorically, the variety of fruit is the diversity of this group because no one wants a basket of just apples. Only one taste = only one thought' (relating it to a business setting).

The discussion

The discussion needs to go right back to what inclusion and diversity means to members of the group. But first, they need to be honest about why they have attended your session. Below is a simple exercise to test this. Ask the following.

Exercise

I am here because. . .

- I want to learn and raise my own awareness.
- I feel I ought to attend.
- I need to be seen to do something as a leader.
- I am eager to be part of the change that is happening around me.

By ticking one of the above (confidentially and individually), they can become conscious of their reason. You will also be able to find out how often they engage in the I&D conversation with family/friends/work colleagues by asking them to choose one of the following statements:

- I never have the I&D conversation.
- I sometimes have the I&D conversation.
- I often engage in the I&D conversation.
- I engage in the I&D conversation every day.

Once you have tested their engagement, below are some questions you can consider to get the conversation started:

- What is your understanding of diversity?
- What is your understanding of inclusion?
- What does inclusion and diversity mean to your organisation?
- What changes have you seen over the past 12 months generally related to I&D?
- How diverse do you believe your organisation is?
- What is something that you love about the culture at your organisation?
- Is there something you do not like about the culture at your organisation?
- How do your customers perceive your organisation around this topic?
- What do your customers expect from your organisation around this topic?

▶

- What do you hear (if anything) about what your competitors are doing in this space?
- What do your employees expect from you as a leadership team in relation to I&D?
- What do you think your employees say about working at your organisation?
- What characteristics and behaviours are most valued and rewarded at your organisation?
- Do employees feel they can approach you as a leader with an I&D issue?
- Have you observed non-inclusive behaviours and what was your reaction to them?

This discussion can last for around two to three hours. Starting with these types of questions enables leaders to begin to challenge their thinking around their own understanding and how they are feeling about the topic.

After the initial discussion, probe their thinking a bit further. For example, ask them questions about themselves, not about the environment around them.

Encourage them to write down their honest answers to the questions below and only share the information they are comfortable with. They may be surprised at what they write; this is their own learning to see what they are prepared to share. The questions below are examples of how to help them think more deeply about themselves:

- What does diversity mean to me?
- What does inclusion mean to me?
- What role do I currently play in the I&D journey?
- Do I feel comfortable being myself at work as a leader?
- Do I show vulnerability as a leader?
- When have I experienced exclusion?
- When have I experienced inclusion?
- Are there aspects of my social identity that I feel I need to keep separate from the workplace?

With the questions listed, aim to create a discussion on how they answered, so they can learn from each other and raise their own awareness of the topic. For example, in answer to the first question, 'What does diversity mean to me?', people will have different opinions; by sharing them, you are creating a learning environment. People may feel less comfortable in answering some of the questions than others, for example 'Do I show vulnerability as a leader?' This may need to be explained, so share an example, such as a leader sharing part of their personal life, talking about a situation that may be difficult or new to them. These examples will help leaders come up with their own answer.

They may not say anything at all, which means you will need to go into greater detail about what the question means. For example, for 'Have I experienced exclusion?', you could use an example such as the school playground: the child who is left out of a group. Share some of your own personal stories too as the facilitator. Trust the process: there will always be someone who is happy to share their story, so let them share, but ensure others have the time and space to get comfortable with sharing their answer. People will need a different amount of time and space before sharing, so enable the space, and be comfortable with silence: this is their thinking time.

You want to simply create a learning environment, where leaders can raise their awareness and feel comfortable in talking about uncomfortable topics. I&D can be emotive and highly sensitive, but the learning can be rich. Getting the conversation on the table is a step that cannot be missed out.

At the end of the discussion, ensure you close the discussion down and don't leave anything sensitive or left unfinished. Remind everyone of the agreed way of working you set up at the beginning and ask if everyone is comfortable as they may have gone through some uncomfortable thinking. Remind them that it is good to be stretched. You may wish to use the method shown in Figure 13.1.

It can be explained that many of us have a tendency to stay in our comfort zone, being comfortable with what we know, surrounding ourselves with people we are comfortable with. This is not necessarily where the real learning takes place. Most of our learning occurs in the 'stretch zone'. Here, we are stretching our thinking, bringing some unconscious thinking to the conscious mind and testing it, becoming aware of many of our thoughts that we are likely to have accessed for the first time or for the first time in a very long while. It is not healthy to move into a panic zone, where we may find ourselves slightly out of control and unsafe. Looking at this 'zones' model is a helpful way to close the conversation and ask where everyone feels they are.

As you close, you need some form of outcome; you want members of the group to think about their own commitments to I&D and how they would like to be engaged as a leader. Ask them to make two personal commitments as they leave

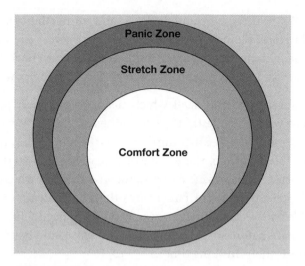

Figure 13.1 Comfort, stretch and panic zone

Source: Based on Ryan and Markova, The Comfort Stretch
Panic model, 2006.

the session (see Table 13.1). Remind them that they need to be visible in this
topic and it is part of their role to do so. It is not an 'add-on'; it is simply part of
their everyday action and behavioural patterns.

Leaders may be unsure about what commitments to make, so they may need
prompting. For example, they might choose to:

● be an executive sponsor for one of the network groups in the organisation

● do a 'lunch and learn'/'townhall'/panel discussion on the topic and talk
about their own experiences. This can show authenticity and sometimes
vulnerability which is something people love to see.

Be aware that this may be the first time that leaders will have engaged and pos-
sibly shown some vulnerability in this topic, so they will need to be guided. If

Table 13.1 Ask participants to note down personal commitments

Personal commitments
Commitment 1 I will. . .
Commitment 2 I will. . .

they declare they would like to be an executive sponsor for a particular group, they will need a brief and guidance to know what their role is likely to be as a sponsor.

In summary, never underestimate the importance of bringing the conversation to the leaders. This must be done with respect and understanding that just because they are leaders it does not mean they know much about I&D. They may even feel that every word they say will be scrutinised, and if they build a fear around what could happen, they will avoid the conversation altogether. Give them the time and respect they deserve. I have met very few leaders who simply do not want to learn about this topic.

It can be lonely as a leader, so when we can break down any barriers and see them as human beings who want to learn about this topic, it narrows the gap between leaders and other employees lower down the organisation. It is important for them to become more conscious and aware of their own actions/behaviours and of other people's actions/behaviours around them, and of how they might be perceived by others.

Encourage them to hold each other accountable regarding their own commitments, discuss how they can continue their engagement in the I&D conversation and ask each other and their direct reports about inclusion and diversity.

One way to do this is to add 15 minutes to their leadership agenda and ask each leader to provide an update on how they are progressing against the personal commitments they made during the session. If they do not have time to do this, question their commitment to I&D.

CHAPTER 14
ATTRACTING, DEVELOPING AND RETAINING TALENT

The employees – the talent – are the engine of organisations. When focusing on talent with an I&D lens, it is best to split it into three areas. Look at how your organisation

- attracts talent
- develops talent
- retains talent.

Your main partners in these three areas are the Chief People Officer (CPO), who manages the whole process, and other leaders who are likely to report into them, such as: Head of Talent, Head of Reward and Head of Leadership Development. These roles may be split even further, such as: Head of Talent Acquisition (the Attract component) and Head of Talent Management/Leadership and Development (the Develop and Retain components).

These stakeholders will hold the key to unlocking the potential to have more diverse talent across the organisation. Let us start with Attract.

Attracting talent

The first things to review are where your talent comes from, how are you attracting talent into your organisation and what mechanisms you have in place. Once you have reviewed these, you will then be able to determine the levels of diversity that are being attracted to the organisation and the points where diverse talent enters.

Attracting talent at entry level

Let us start at entry level. It may be an individual's first role in the world of work. The organisation may have a graduate scheme, in which case you should stipulate that you want to see diversity in the candidate shortlists. Watch for bias. For example, if an organisation has a stipulation of only taking in those who have achieved a first-class degree, be aware of the consequences of doing this. The stipulation could be limiting diversity from the outset.

There are groups of talented individuals who may not have gone to university or did not achieve a first but can bring as much, if not more, to your organisation.

Look at other schemes that bring in other types of talent from different backgrounds who have great skillsets that your organisation may require, rather than promoting a narrow view of 'must have gone to university/must have achieved a first'. Think about the percentage of this group versus the talent your organisation is excluding.

Attracting talent can be like a funnel, starting with a wide top, but the more stipulations (potential biases) you put in the funnel, the narrower it becomes, filtering out diverse talent along the way.

Attracting talent at senior level

To search for senior talent, internal and external recruiters need to understand what the diversity focus is when searching, in addition to the skillsets required. To equip them, they need to see how I&D fits into their search. For example, if the organisation has a target to attract more women into senior leadership positions, then recruiters will need to search for more women and have them on the shortlist to present to the organisation. Equally the organisation should provide guidelines for recruiters, so they understand what the diversity requirements are. Any diversity targets need to be shared so recruiters are aware of them and can provide a diverse shortlist of candidates that help towards the target.

Below is a template to educate and upskill recruiters so they can learn about the I&D efforts. It is helpful to start at the beginning and understand why I&D is important to the organisation:

What does inclusion and diversity mean to our organisation?

● Diversity is valuing and promoting differences and unique characteristics.

● Inclusion is empowering individuals by creating an inclusive environment in the workplace.

● A diverse workforce thinks in different ways, has different approaches, bringing different skills, experience and knowledge to create even greater success.

Why is inclusion and diversity important to us?

● Globalisation has brought diversity into our everyday lives.

● We aim to recruit diverse talent into key decision-making roles so that we have a better understanding of our customers and employees.

● By continuing to build a diverse and talented workforce we will drive innovation, build our customer awareness and increase our productivity, all of which are important to us if we are to remain at the cutting edge and competitive in the market.

It is also good to map this back to values and/or behaviours your organisation may have, so recruiters can see how these fit together.

Next, you want to be clear on your diversity priorities and goals. Ensure the recruiters understand these goals. For example, if your goals are to increase diversity, you may want to stipulate the following.

Our I&D priorities

● Our aim is to increase diversity in leadership positions. Our criterion is the quality of the candidate, and we expect to see a diverse range of candidates from different backgrounds.

● We aim for each senior leader to achieve a greater balance of diversity in their team. Therefore, if applicants from similar backgrounds are shortlisted it is important that we understand why, so that we can increase our knowledge and insight into diversity and ensure that we are being really challenging with our sourcing.

The above is very general, but you can focus on specific diversity groups or themes, such as internationality.

Internationality

- We operate in a variety of countries, presenting us with a diverse culture. We want to increase the number of people who have experience of working across nationalities and cultures. Diverse leadership teams make better decisions, and building teams that have a global and diverse background will drive strategic advantage.

- As we are an international organisation, the ability to speak more than one language is becoming increasingly important, specifically in the countries where we operate.

The next step is to ensure recruiters are held accountable for attracting and seeking out diverse talent. The following guidelines will help set expectations:

- To create a diverse and inclusive environment, we need to reflect that in our recruitment and retention of employees.

- We need to go over and above to seek out the best talent, and we expect hirers to provide instructions to their agencies, to seek talent using an inclusion and diversity lens.

- We need to ensure we are inclusive with all candidates, regardless of gender, disability, sexual orientation, age, race, ethnicity and nationality.

The above list can also be adapted for hiring managers, who will require upskilling in inclusion and diversity when hiring.

Reaching diverse groups

When looking to reach diverse groups, such as gender, disability, sexual orientation, age, race, ethnicity and nationality, you need to provide clear communications that are accessible and understandable to the widest audience. Candidates look for inclusion so the more inclusive you make your job advertising the better. For example, aim for simplicity and promote details around the benefits of working in the organisation, such as:

- flexible working
- inclusive company culture
- Employee Resource Groups and networks.

Avoid:

- complexity
- being a demanding company

- being an unappealing company
- corporate jargon that means nothing outside of your organisation.

Use inclusive words and language:

- collaborate
- creative
- curious
- imaginative
- intuitive
- empathy
- partnering
- encouraging
- supportive
- connected
- transparent.

Ensure job adverts are personal and inclusive so the reader feels you are talking to them; for example:

- Use the word 'you' not 'them'.
- Be precise and direct.
- Simplify, rather than using lengthy narrative.
- Avoid using the word 'fit'.
- Avoid asking for x number of years' experience.

The talent acquisition team – the 'recruiter'

It is important to equip and educate the talent acquisition team, so they are aware of the importance of I&D in their process. First, it is important to understand what the relationship is with their hiring managers, how they take a brief and what the expectations of them are. Let us start with the relationship:

- Recruiters cannot be subservient to the hiring manager – they need to work in partnership, enabling them to challenge the hiring manager's thinking and support the I&D mission.

- They are able to identify and challenge non-inclusive behaviours and language while discussing the brief with the hiring manager.
- They have a set of objective questions and have evidence-based discussions to present to the hiring manager.
- They can guide the hiring manager, demonstrate that they are looking for diversity that enables and enhances the organisation to obtain different perspectives and offerings.

The hiring manager

Hiring managers also hold the key to unlocking diversity. Hiring agencies and talent acquisition teams can bring as much diversity as they like to the door of the hiring manager, but if the hiring manager is not opening the door to diverse candidates, then the process fails.

Hiring managers may be up against time pressure, needing to fill the role fast, and thinking there might be a business risk of having an empty role, so they want to recruit fast. They may also look for someone who will 'fit' into the team. Both can be detrimental to the organisation: the quick hire may result in bringing in someone who is of a similar ilk to the rest of the team, while the 'good fit' may not bring different skillsets to the team.

Upskilling and making the hiring manager aware of potential biases and challenges will enable them to have a more balanced approach to selecting candidates. Biases they should look out for when considering candidates include:

- where they live
- age
- names that might be unusual to the hiring manager
- career breaks on CVs
- level of qualification
- health declarations
- marital status.

Reviewing and assessing candidates

Once the hiring manager has received a shortlist of candidates, it is important to review candidates against consistent selection criteria, not against each other. Asking the same interview questions with standard evaluation forms will help with objectivity.

The interview process

When interviewing, hiring managers need to be aware of biases. A candidate may be selected because the hiring manager gravitates to them more than to others: for example, the candidate may remind the hiring manager of themselves or they have gone to the same school. This may distract from their core skillsets and competencies. To avoid this, the more diverse the interview panel, the better. Some organisations stipulate that they would like to have at least two women on the candidate shortlist, or two women on the interview panel. It is better to address this by simply ensuring the panel is diverse. Use simple guidelines to make up a diverse interview panel – this takes the focus away from tokenism such as 'I want to ask you to be part of this interview panel because you are a woman'. Below is an example of guidelines that an organisation can put in place:

- Approach panellists and explain they are being asked because of their background, skillsets and knowledge.
- Ensure it is done in a collaborative way such as an email out to all the panellists at once.
- Enable the panellists to see they are being invited because of their diversity of thought and style, and what everyone can bring to the panel.

Sara Hill, Founder and CEO of Role Mapper Technologies, a platform to design and manage inclusive jobs that unlock talent and diversity.

Sara: *The interview process, if not managed correctly, leaves you wide open to biases that impact how you conduct the interview and the hiring decisions you make. In the world of bias-academia, the 'halo or horns' effect is a term often used to describe specifically how 'confirmatory bias' can manifest itself in the recruitment process – when an interviewer allows one strong point about the candidate to overshadow or have an effect on everything else. For instance, knowing they used to work at a particular company might be looked upon favourably. Everything the applicant says during the interview is seen in this light: 'Well, she left out an important part of the answer to that question, but, she must know it, she used to work at x company.' The 'horns' effect is just the opposite – allowing one weak point to influence everything else. And then there is the 'mini-me' bias, where we have an unconscious tendency to favour those who remind us of ourselves. This can result in managers favouring a candidate because they are similar to themselves rather than because they are the best person for the job.*

Clarity on requirements is the key to structured interviewing: what you are assessing – the requirements – and ensuring the criteria you are assessing against are inclusive and have been reviewed for bias. Ultimately, to ensure your structured interview is inclusive you only want to be assessing the absolute essential criteria required to perform well in the job; desirable criteria are not discussed.

Without a structured interview process, managers may well fall foul of their unconscious biases in their interpretation, assessment and selection of talent. But if the requirements you are assessing have not been rigorously assessed for bias, or potential to exclude talent, then all your efforts may well be in vain.

Break interviewer bias with intelligent job design

So, how do you ensure requirements are inclusive? It is during the process of designing a job and creating a job description that you determine the screening and assessment criteria for prospective candidates.

By adopting an intelligent job design approach you connect the dots with your inclusive job description, your inclusive requirements and your inclusive structured interview process.

At the point at which you are creating the job – whether for job profiling, job description creation, job advert creation – you design your requirements inclusively and ensure that they feed into a structured interview, closing the loop and de-biasing the process.

The candidate experience

Candidates will feel something when they go through the interview process and will make a judgement about how they are treated. It is important to see candidates as 'customers'. Treat them with respect and show them that, despite the outcome, they were valued in the process.

It is important to be clear with the candidate and lay out the process and expectations of the organisation:

● *Define what types of selection process are appropriate: CV sifting, interview, psychometrics, presentation, case study etc.*

● *Be realistic about the necessary stages in the process.*

Assessing the candidates

It is important to be consistent. For example, if you have five candidates you are interviewing, use simple criteria that enable you to score everyone the same, the same questions and the same scoring structure. This enables you to compare each of them based on an aligned system, which means the scoring is fair and equal.

● *Define clear evidence-points against the evaluation of each individual candidate.*

● *Rate candidates in relation to evidence not personal preference.*

● *Observe what they say and do.*

● *Classify each bit of evidence against each capability required for the role.*

● *Evaluate and score the candidates equally and against each of the capabilities based on the evidence to ensure everyone is treated fairly and equally.*

Retaining and developing talent

It is important to know who you are retaining and who is being developed. This kind of data can demonstrate to the organisation where the trends are; for example, if you did an exercise to identify the types of talent that leave the organisation versus who is staying, you may find strong evidence and trends.

Identifying talent

Many organisations have a talent process. This talent data will provide you with the evidence you need to identify who is being developed and promoted into the next big role, and who is not.

Talent reviews are usually held to discuss senior roles and ensure the organisation is future-ready to continue creating growth. A talent review is usually held with the senior leader managing the senior roles, along with their 'Head of HR'.

The talent review meeting

First, ensure that the talent review panel is made up of a diverse mix of leaders. At the beginning of each talent review meeting, conduct a 10- to 15-minute discussion on 'How to conduct an inclusive talent review', setting the landscape for an equal and balanced discussion. It is recommended that you invite an impartial person who can help conduct this, such as the I&D practitioner. This will help to:

- Raise awareness of how bias interferes with talent selection.

- Give each other permission to call out non-inclusive behaviours and comments that may be seen to be assuming. Remind each other to stick with objective, evidence-based discussions, which help to remove any assumptions.

- Strip out unconscious bias, and be consciously aware of any biases that may play out.

- Ask questions throughout the talent review to ensure you are checking that you are setting yourselves up for a successful discussion.

Below is an example of a set of guidelines that can be used.

Talent review guidelines

The following checklist will enable diverse and balanced conversations during the review, allowing you to become more knowledgeable about every unique individual that has the potential to progress, and removing any assumptions about others so that all the interviewees have an equal chance of progression. It is important to understand the barriers that exist. The checklist below can help create an evidence-based discussion:

- Given the talent mix on the current team, what does this person bring that is new or unique?

- By adding them, what would the team look like in terms of diverse skillsets?

- Does this person remind me of someone else?

- Am I shifting criteria to fit a preferred candidate?

- Am I resisting a candidate because their profile is not what I am used to seeing?

- Do I feel an obligation to this individual that is influencing how I am discussing them?

- Am I leaning towards this person because I was over-influenced by our last interaction?

- Was this person associated with a big success which casts a halo around my view of them? Do I really understand the contribution they made and what that implies for future performance?

- Do I know more about one of the individuals than the others? Is this extra knowledge making me more, or less, positive than I should be?

- If the identified front runner is not available, who else would we consider?

- Instead of thinking who could do the role best, should we think about how different people would do the job – that is, what would it take for them to be successful?

Inclusion nudge

'Change the default questions, from: When is the candidate ready, to: The candidate is ready now. This enables leaders to argue: why not, rather than: why?'

How well do you know your talent?

It is important to widen leadership visibility across the full talent pipeline, so leaders have equal knowledge of everyone they plan to discuss. It is also important to fill the knowledge gap so that you can make a more inclusive decision, rather than make a decision in the talent review when you do not really know some of the talent that well. Those individuals who are more visible and better known may have an advantage. Make an action to commit to getting to know the others better over time. The following are real examples of assumptions that I have heard in talent reviews:

'Difficult to say what the future holds, don't know her that well'

'I don't think she will come back after her career break'

'I don't really know this individual'

The I&D practitioner's role

The I&D practitioner, if present in the review, needs to be clear to the rest of the panel what their role is and what they are looking out for. Set the role up as follows:

- I am here to set out the guidance so we can all 'slot' our diversity lens in and have objective conversations and make decisions that are right for the organisation, rather than ourselves.
- I shall take notes to encourage a learning experience after the panel, enabling us to continue to upskill ourselves and improve our methods.
- I will act as an advisor and call out any assumptions that are made. This will encourage a learning environment while we are going through the talent review.

The I&D practitioner will be looking for what the data tells them.

- What is the make-up of the individuals sitting on the succession chart, the high potential list or the talent grid?
- Is the organisation making progress in working towards any diversity targets? For example, if you have a target to increase representation of women at the senior level and there are no women in the organisation who are in a position to move up to that level, there is a problem.

Here are more real-life examples of assumptions that should not be made:

'She is very emotional'

'She is a perfectionist'

'She has her kids, quite rightly, she won't want to move'

The I&D practitioner should aim to present a report to the panel post-talent review with observations that may need respectfully calling out. Discussing the changes to behaviour that need to be made to improve future talent reviews will enable a learning environment so that everyone can continue to improve.

This enables the panel of leaders to recognise their own behaviours, so they can aim to:

- retain and develop the best in the market and become an employer of choice

- have an inclusive recruitment and retention process in place that promotes diversity of thought in leadership, offering more innovative solutions
- identify diverse talent, and have access to a wider talent pool to help the organisation evolve
- address how to deal with the barriers and biases they do not realise they put in place.

If they ignore this, it becomes a risk to the organisation for these reasons:

- It will lack diversity of thought in critical decision-making meetings.
- It will not be an attractive place to work as a result of homogeneity and lack of diverse role models.
- It will lack the ability to problem solve.
- It will lack innovation.
- It will provide an 'exclusive' place to work, rather than an 'inclusive' place to work.
- It will reduce diversity of teams, impacting the ability to perform and reflect customers, with the risk of losing them.

Watching out for inclusive and non-inclusive language

It is important to be aware of the language being used and how questions and statements are framed. When questions are reframed, a different answer may arise. For example, try asking 'Could they do the job?' rather than 'How would they successfully do the job?'

Getting the organisation future-ready with an I&D lens

It is important to accept and understand where the organisation is now and where it wants to get to. Focus the discussion on how the talent pipeline is going to build over time to achieve a more diverse talent pool which contains a broader skillset to draw from.

Consider setting subtle targets for promotions and successors. Below are examples on setting targets.

Succession plans:

- 50 per cent female/male gender diversity, up to and including job level x
- at least x women on succession chart at job level x.

Promotions:

- at least as many promotions for women as for men, up to and including job level x
- at least 40 per cent female promotions at job level x.

A timeline will need to be added, and this should reflect the current position and how long realistically it will take to achieve a diverse talent pool that can be represented throughout the top end of the pipeline. Below is an example of setting a timeline against the target:

1. Achieve x% M/x% F by 2022
2. Achieve x% M/x% F by 2023
3. Achieve x% M/x% F by 2024

Figure 14.1 provides a visual for leaders to see the current state of play. This can lead to a conversation about how long it will take for the organisation to achieve gender balance.

Another way to show visually where you are now is illustrated in Figure 14.2.

Some other questions to challenge leaders' thinking can be:

- Who were the last three people you hired?
- Who was the last person you promoted?
- Who is the top performer in your team?
- Who is the bottom performer in your team?
- What are the demographics of these people? What is similar and what might be missing (a blind spot) that could hinder success?
- What steps are you taking on a day-to-day basis to bring in a more diverse workforce? For example, if the organisation has a target of 40/60 per cent

female/male representation at senior level, what action are you taking on a daily basis to work towards (or against) the target?

Succession plan (example)

ROLE 1	
Name:	
Role start	x x
Date started	x x
Successors now–18 months	
Successors 18 months–3 years	
Successors 3–5 years	

ROLE 2	
Name	
Role start	x x
Date started	x x
Successors now–18 months	
Successors 18 months–3 years	
Successors 3–5 years	

ROLE 3	
Name	
Role start	x x
Date started	x x
Successors now–18 months	
Successors 18 months–3 years	
Successors 3–5 years	

Figure 14.1 An example of a succession plan

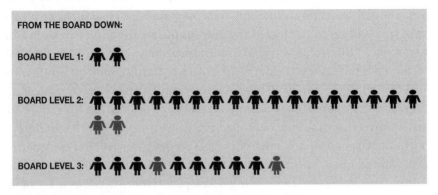

Figure 14.2 Example: visualising the current state of play

I&D and high potential lists

It is important to ensure high potentials are invested in and mobilised. This could mean offering them a stretch assignment, putting them on a succession plan or promoting them with financial reward. These examples may sound obvious, but some organisations have high potentials sitting dormant on a list. The following questions could help the organisation invest in high potentials:

- How long have the individuals been sitting on the list?
- What has happened with their career since they made the list?
- Who do we not know well enough?
- Who do we risk losing?

Leaders need to get to know their high potentials and learn about their personal aspirations, not just the organisation's. This will help them better understand whether the individual is stretched enough, fulfilled and happy in the role they are currently doing. It also presents the opportunity of identifying if the high potential is supported – they may be missing a mentor, or a sponsor who is looking out for them in relation to further opportunities.

Leadership and development (L&D) programmes

It is a good idea to do a review of who the organisation invests in, with leadership and development programmes. What is the diversity of individuals that are invited on leadership and development programmes? This will be an indication of who is likely to get the next big roles as the organisation invests in L&D programmes. Also, review the L&D training programme's content with an I&D lens. For example, is it a one-day outdoor team-building course, or a residential course over three to five days? These examples may be more attractive to certain groups and their appeal may depend on ability to attend. If a team-building event is planned, ensure it is suitable and inclusive for everyone. It is important to focus on who can attend, otherwise L&D programmes will be developed for a select few groups. Consider putting targets on the attendee list so conscious decisions are made as to who is being developed. If there is a diverse list of talent, ensure those who accept are diverse, so it does not become only a majority group who accept.

Performance ratings

Another review to undertake is performance ratings. For example, you may find that women's performance ratings are higher than men's, but when it comes to salary increases, they may not get a higher salary increase. Good practice is to do an audit of performance ratings against salary reviews and assess the balance and equity.

Martell and colleagues (1996) found that just a 1 per cent higher performance rating for men led to a 35 per cent female to 65 per cent male imbalance at the top level of one organisation.

Outcomes to look for

- A greater awareness of biases and assumptions when making hiring and promotion decisions
- An understanding of the risk of homogeneity in teams and the larger organisation
- Awareness of specific individuals who are more likely to be excluded or not discussed.

Further resources

Interview

Sara Hill, Founder and CEO, Role Mapper Technologies.

Publications

Martell, R. F., Lane, D. M. and Emrich, C. (1996). Male–Female Differences: A Computer Simulation. http://www.ruf.rice.edu/~lane/papers/male_female.pdf

Nielsen, T. and Kepinski, L. (2016). *Inclusion Nudges Guidebook*, p. 145.

CHAPTER 15
BRINGING CUSTOMERS AND SUPPLIERS ON THE JOURNEY

In this chapter we will discuss how to bring customers and suppliers on the journey, and how to have conversations enabling your organisation to be more mindful and inclusive of your customers and suppliers.

Customers

The more aware we are of our customers' diverse needs, the greater the relationship we will build with them. It is obvious that a great way to treat your customers is to build a relationship, but without being mindful of their diverse needs, there may be blind spots that prevent you from growing the relationship.

Below is a real example of a male leader talking through his moments of realisation:

> I walked into the sales pitch and realised in that moment that I had brought my five white male colleagues with me and we all sat down in front of the customer who was female. I did not think about it until I was presented with the situation.

> I always hugged my client when I met her, one time I chose not to, I noticed that she felt much more comfortable and the meeting was one of the best I ever had.

It is not about right or wrong, it is much more about being conscious of the present situation and the comfort of other people when meeting. Just being aware and conscious of your own behaviour can lead you to better understand how you might be able to grow the relationship with your customer or lose it.

Below are a couple of examples where companies brought a different and more inclusive way of thinking to their business.

B2C (business-to-customer) example

An organisation I worked with had stores across the country with customers coming in to buy a product. The store assistants used too much jargon and they gravitated too much to a particular type of customer. They were unaware of the customers they were excluding.

The goal was to become more inclusive in their style and language, creating a more inclusive store design and gravitating to all customers, not just those they were comfortable dealing with. As a result of this, over a short period it was noticeable that store profits increased, because the customer base broadened once other demographics were no longer excluded. The impact before this exercise was that the marketing and communications team were taking data from these stores and building their target markets around current sales. Therefore, even in the marketing and advertising, the impact of excluding customers (unintentional blind spots) was having an impact on performance and profitability. This also had a knock-on effect on their advertising, in that it only spoke to one segment. Later on, as this more inclusive customer approach was taken into account the company's market segment and advertising changed.

A completely different sector: when I worked with an online platform selling fashion, they began to recognise that their representation of different types of people was non-existent. Caroline Casey, Founder of The Valuable 500, stated in an article in *Forbes* magazine:

> More clothes are made for dogs than those with disabilities, with the rigid size structures routinely shutting out 1 in 5 people.
>
> **(Casey 2020)**

B2B (business-to-business) example

I worked with a business where consultants were assigned to a client's office and worked on long-term projects. After reviewing this, it was found that one or two clients were bullying the consultants who were contracted into their offices.

This is where your organisation needs to take a stand and decide what is ok and what is not ok in the interests of your own talent.

This can be discussed and addressed at the pitch stage, stating ethical standards that you have as an organisation. Reference to I&D at the pitch stage puts you in a strong position to begin raising awareness of how you value I&D. For example, in this case:

● Treat consultants with dignity and respect, regardless of their background.

● Be inclusive of all, regardless of employment status, giving everyone the opportunity to share views and opinions to help make the project a success.

Whether customers and clients are B2C or B2B, you have a great opportunity to bring the I&D conversation to them, discussing the value of it and enabling a better understanding of each other's views on the topic.

Things you may wish to share with your customers are:

● Your I&D annual report.

● Your diverse representation, and the efforts – for example, setting targets – you are making to bring diversity into decision-making teams, and senior roles.

● The efforts you are making to attract diverse talent and the partnerships you have to help make this happen. You may have examples where you partner with diverse recruitment agencies to help attract more people from a particular diversity group (RARE Recruitment in the UK (promoting great talent from the Black community) is a great example of this).

I&D commercial opportunities with your customer

Depending on your industry and what your organisation does, you may have an opportunity to commercialise your I&D efforts, and sell your solutions. For example, a data research organisation can offer I&D research to help other companies become more aware of I&D and to understand their own business and its baseline, with topics such as women in the workplace, diversity and globalisation.

You may have a new product on the market which has been designed from an inclusion perspective, thus making it a more accessible and sellable product.

All customers are unique. One size does not fit all. You can help your own organisation and your customers, by following this simple checklist when considering I&D in customer-facing initiatives:

- Business rationale:
  - Profile current and potential customers and their spending power, and collect good practices from benchmarking.
- Customer intelligence:
  - Check for unconscious bias in beliefs about current and potential customer segments.
- Marketing images:
  - Review current marketing materials and campaigns for realistic images of current and future customers.
- Focus groups:
  - Listen to what various diverse market groups say about your company and its products and services.
- Product innovation:
  - Involve and engage with diverse customers during the development of new products and services.
- Leverage knowledge of internal Employee Resource Groups:
  - Ask ERGs to contribute to new market/product growth.
- Goals:
  - Set I&D targets for leaders around capturing market share among diversity groups.

You could use a 'From. . . To. . . ' model, which would help you improve in your customer I&D (Table 15.1).

Advertising

Advertising has become increasingly diverse in its representation. This gives more people the ability to connect to others that are from similar backgrounds or that have had similar experiences. Yet, I still see advertisements

Table 15.1 An example of a 'From. . . To. . .' model

FROM	TO
One size fits all – UNIVERSAL	More awareness and understanding of the INDIVIDUAL need
EXCESSIVE selling to hit commission	What is the customer need? Match customer preference and explain how it can benefit their lives
Talking JARGON to customers	Use all-encompassing, inclusive language
Too much choice – CONFUSED	Give fewer choices/the right choice, working to the individual specification
CLOSED question: 'Can I help you?'	OPEN question: 'How can I help you?'

and campaigns that are offensive or biased. Poor judgement on advertising can lead to brands losing out because a perceived 'quick and funny' joke is actually offensive to segments of the market.

This is where you can help your customer to understand the commercial value of I&D, making them aware of the benefits of improving the way they communicate to their audience and of improving diversity across their organisation.

I have personally experienced being ignored by sales representatives because of how I have been dressed. As a sports person, I only had time to buy a new car after my match on a Saturday and went to the car showroom of a popular brand of car in my sports kit. I could not get served. Three weeks in a row I went and each time the receptionist promised that someone would call me or told me to come back another day. In the end I gave up trying. On talking to someone who worked for the said brand, I was told that the sales staff enjoy dealing with people who are dressed more smartly as they make an assumption about social status and perceive their chance of a sale as being higher. They even google customers' addresses to see if it is worth dealing with them based on where they live. I actually already owned this brand of car and was looking to upgrade it. Needless to say I bought another make of car and will not go back to the brand who ignored me.

It is not ok to exclude any customer, because their image may not reflect their spending power! This is critical when looking objectively at market segmentation and untapped markets.

The I&D practitioner

It is very common for the I&D practitioner to have an internal focus, but by moving the agenda further to think about the customer, you can influence and educate the other areas of your organisation to be more inclusive in their areas of work. This is how you can get the whole engine to work, and the internal practices can enhance the external and vice versa.

'Will the internal piece ever be achieved?' I speak to organisations who tell me, 'I would like to sort out the internal piece before thinking about the customer and the external I&D opportunities.' My response... 'Will the internal piece ever be achieved?'

They are complementary so ideally do both in parallel – internal and external. This does not mean you have to tell the external world, especially your customers, that you are a leader in this topic. You can continue to aspire to do better, and just let your customers know that you are on a journey and aim to improve both internally and externally. By doing this, you can begin to help your customers along the journey too. You will find that many customers will be impressed with your aspiration of doing better.

A great way to include your customers in the debate is to hold webinars, forums and events where you bring together a range of customers, employees and voices from the NGO (not-for-profit) community or the industry and have the conversation. The dialogue can be very educational and rewarding as your customers will be inspired and educated to want to do more for their own organisation. They will remember that it was your organisation who helped them get on the journey. This contributes to the business case of helping your customers, building the relationship with them through inclusion and diversity.

As there is a growing expectation that organisations will have I&D high on their agenda, your customers will be very grateful that you are helping them to do something about it. As well as being good for business, it is the right thing to do.

Setting suppliers' expectations

As an organisation you are likely to have suppliers serving your organisation. Equally, you are likely to be a supplier to your own clients in some form.

Whichever, it is important to know the suppliers you are using, and your own supply chain management.

This is critical for your ethical standards and reputation: if you are not ethical in your supplier operations, you will get found out and it could be leaked to the media. You may lose clients, employees and leaders if you are hiding anything that is unethical. Do not do anything you would not want to see in the media. In 2020, fashion retailer Boohoo was in the news relating to the treatment of its workers in one of its UK factories. It was accused of paying below the minimum wage. One serious incident such as this could damage all the great inclusion and diversity work that has been built across an organisation. Boohoo took quick action and held an investigation into its supply chain. If your supply chain links are not transparent, you could be in danger of becoming the next Boohoo. Trust and ethical practices are increasingly important as employees and customers expect these. The first step is to ensure your organisation has processes that proactively look for any issues.

Inclusion and diversity needs to be in as many interventions across the organisation as possible. One likely area is in an intervention within sales. Sales will build a proposal, in order to win business from potential clients. This is a great way to promote the efforts that your organisation has been making in I&D, and at the same time raise awareness among the sales team selling to customers, as your customers may tell others about your I&D efforts.

Be prepared to have a statement that defines your efforts around inclusion and diversity. For example:

> 'We actively work towards fostering inclusive behaviours and bringing diverse perspectives to opportunities and challenges. We aim to attract, retain and develop a diverse mix of talented individuals to create an inclusive culture in our organisation so we can better serve our customers, with the diversity of thinking and difference in our backgrounds that bring us to more innovative and creative solutions. We believe that a truly inclusive culture is created by promoting active conversations around various aspects that our people and customers believe in.'

This demonstrates your commitment to I&D.

Further resources

Casey, C. (2020). 'What to wear: the missing voice in the fashion industry'. *Forbes* magazine, 22 September. https://www.forbes.com/sites/carolinecasey/2020/09/22/what-to-wearthe-missing-voice-in-the-fashion-industry/?sh=1e823af11086

Financial Times (2020). 'Boohoo has "significant issues" in its supply chain, review finds', 25 September. https://www.ft.com/content/3cc4acc9-3f8a-4fb8-90e5-9a70116df7d4

CONCLUSION

I dedicate this book to all the truly amazing I&D practitioners out there. The profession has grown so quickly and roles are opening up everywhere. It is about time, but I&D practitioners enter the profession because they want to make a difference, make a positive impact on society. Sadly, most operate with too few resources, too small a budget and their own job level is sometimes middle management, which does not have the gravitas it deserves.

Organisations' expectations of I&D are greater than the commitment they are prepared to put behind it. Anyone who wants to enter the profession, I respect you. The skillset required is pure hard work, dedication to the cause, with a lot of influencing skills and drive. I&D practitioners endlessly nudge the agenda forward. Often, their stakeholders are difficult, lack understanding and challenge (usually challenging the data).

I hope this book has empowered the I&D profession and reminds each and every one of us that we are making a difference. I&D professionals are supportive of each other and recognise that through collaboration it does not have to be such a lonely place out there.

I hope this book gives you the freedom to really challenge and hold your organisation accountable. It is about having the tough conversation, holding the mirror up and asking:

- What do you really want to achieve?
- What commitment are you really going to give to this?
- How serious are you as a leader, leading your organisation?
- Why are you doing this?

If there is a misalignment between the I&D practitioner's ambition and the organisation's, the journey will be an emotional roller coaster. The first question for the I&D practitioner is: What have I got to work with?

What have I got to work with?

As an I&D practitioner, work with what you have and set realistic targets based on what the organisation is ready for.

I have worked for a number of organisations, beginning my I&D career in HR and leading up to a 'Chief Diversity Officer' role, with the opportunity to report into a CEO and sit on his board. My curiosity and education along the way have provided me with immense learning: achieving an MSc in Behavioural Change made me see that it really does start with our own behaviour before we can address inclusion and then embrace diversity (B.I.D.). There is no right or wrong as to how to approach I&D – it is more about how I&D practitioners can make an impact. This needs to be set out at the beginning: If I deliver this approach, what will be the impact?

If I deliver this approach, what will be the impact?

I never stop learning. I have had the privilege of being mentored by a wonderful 33-year-old Black British woman, who shared with me her experiences and talked about her family history in Zimbabwe. For me, as a white British woman, I am so curious to learn about her experiences and those of others where I do not have the experience myself.

I will continue to learn and will not give up caring about this cause. I&D practitioners will have their own reason for entering the profession. It is not an easy profession to get into, but it is a very rewarding one. I entered it many years ago and for a long time was naive about the reality of people's behaviours. I simply had a fixed mindset, believing that there is no reason for treating people disrespectfully and unfairly.

No one gets out of bed in the morning to be disrespected!

I am proud of my naivety in my earlier days – it made me push the I&D agenda with ignorance because I simply held values that were non-negotiable.

I grew up in a female-dominant environment: my mother brought me up, she had her own business, I went to an all girls' school, and lived every spare moment on the netball court, playing for my club, my county and south of England. Along the way, I also had the privilege of having a female teacher as my mentor and role model. I was surrounded by very empowering and powerful women; I was naive about women being unfairly treated for so many years. In my first corporate role I did not understand why there were so few women in decision-making roles.

I do not want my nieces to be paid less than their male counterparts when they enter the workplace. I do not want them to see what I have seen. Yet I have been lucky that my profession has enabled me to be pivotal in making change happen.

Regardless of your background, you have picked this book up for a reason – thank you. You can help make a difference regardless of what you do in life. Please make one commitment: call out the unfairness of the actions you observe.

Call out the unfairness of the actions you observe

The I&D profession continues to rapidly grow, and whether you are entering it or have been in the profession for a while, I know the dedication it takes to nudge things on. It is a tough role, a role in which you are expected to be analytical, present findings, operate with leaders, change behaviour, deal with issues that are found. The list of skillsets goes on. . .

Thank you. Keep going.

INDEX